The Path to Perfection

In the name of Allāh,

Most Gracious Most Merciful.

All praise be to Allāh,

Lord of the Worlds,

and peace and blessings be

upon His Messenger Muḥammad,

Mercy to the Worlds

SHAYKH MASĪḤULLĀH KHĀN

The Path to Perfection

An Edited Anthology of the Spiritual Teachings of Ḥakīm al-Umma Mawlānā Ashraf ʿAlī Thānawī

WHITE THREAD

SANTA BARBARA • CALIFORNIA • USA

First Edition April 2005

ISBN 0-9728358-7-3 (*softcover*)

Published by:
White Thread Press
California USA • Tel: 1 805 968 4666
info@whitethreadpress.com • www.whitethreadpress.com
Distributed in the UK by Azhar Academy Ltd. London
sales@azharacademy.com
Tel: +44 (208) 534 9191

Library of Congress
Cataloging-in-Publication Data

Thānvī, Ashraf ʿAlī.
The path to perfection : an
edited anthology of the spiritual teachings
of Ḥakīm al-umma Mawlānā Ashraf ʿAlī Thānawī /
by Muḥammad Masīḥullāh Khān Sherwānī.—1st ed.
p. cm.
ISBN 0-9728358-7-3 (softcover : alk. paper)
1. Mysticism–Islam. 2. Sufism. I. Masīḥullāh Khān,
Muḥammad, d. 1992. II. Title.
BP189.T524 2005
297.4'4–dc22

2004031089

♾ Printed and bound in the United States of America
on acid-free paper. The paper used in this book meets the minimum
requirement of ANSI/NISO Z39.48-1992 (R 1997) (Permanence of Paper).
The binding material has been chosen for strength and durability.

Cover image of Alhambra castle window from iStockphoto
Cover design by ARM and Ather Ali

Whoever acquires
the wealth of arrival and
attaining the love of Allāh
has acquired it by virtue
of following the Sunna.

—Ḥakīm al-Umma

TRANSLITERATION KEY

ء (أ إ)' (A slight catch in the breath. It is also used to indicate where the *hamza* has been dropped from the beginning of a word.)

ا a, ā

ب b

ت t

ث th (Should be pronounced as the *th* in *thin* or *thirst.*)

ج j

ح ḥ (Tensely breathed *h* sound.)

خ kh (Pronounced like the *ch* in Scottish *loch* with the mouth hollowed to produce a full sound.)

د d

ذ dh (Should be pronounced as the *th* in *this* or *that.*)

ر r

ز z

س s

ش sh

ص ṣ (A heavy *s* pronounced far back in the mouth with the mouth hollowed to produce a full sound.)

ض ḍ (A heavy *d/dh* pronounced far back in the mouth with the mouth hollowed to produce a full sound.)

ط ṭ (A heavy *t* pronounced far back in the mouth with the mouth hollowed to produce a full sound.)

ظ ẓ (A heavy *dh* pronounced far back in the mouth with the mouth hollowed to produce a full sound.)

ع ʿ, ʿa, ʿi, ʿu (Pronounced from the throat.)

غ gh (Pronounced like a throaty French *r* with the mouth hollowed to produce a full sound.)

ف f

ق q (A guttural *q* sound with the mouth hollowed to produce a full sound.)

ك k

ل l

م m

ن n

و w, ū, u.

ه h

ي y, ī, i

Contents

Do not be deceived

if you see a performer of

supernatural feats flying through

the air. Measure him by the standard

of the Sharīʿa—how he adheres to

the commands of the Sharīʿa.

—Bāyazīd Basṭāmī

Publisher's Note

In the name of Allāh, the Most Beneficent, the Most Merciful, and peace and blessings upon His final Messenger, Muḥammad, and upon his Family and Companions.

The abridged translation of the *Sharīʿat & Taṣawwuf* by Shaykh Masīḥulllāh Khān of Jalalabad, India was originally published in South Africa in 1981 by some of his students. It was widely acclaimed in that Shaykh Masīḥullāh Khān was one of the foremost students of Ḥakīm al-Umma Mawlānā Ashraf ʿAlī Thānawī and remained in the company of his shaykh for many years. Today, the students of Ḥakīm al-Umma Mawlānā Thānawī, through the guidance of Shaykh Masīḥullāh and others like him, are present all over the world in countries such as, India, Pakistan, Bangladesh, Afghanistan, Myanmar, South Africa, England, United States, Australia, and Canada, spreading the teachings of Islam and reviving the hearts of many.

Ḥakīm al-Umma was a prolific writer, and as reported by Shaykh ʿAbd al-Fattāḥ Abū Ghudda, the late Syrian scholar, his works amount to more than one thousand (*Qīmat al-zaman ʿinda 'l-ʿulamā'*). Many of these works have been translated into English, Bengali, Persian, and other languages.

This book was selected by White Thread Press for publication because of its rich content, particularly because it highlights the salient features of spirituality and of moving on a spiritual path, the signs of a noble shaykh, the description of blameworthy traits and the means of remedying them, and the description of praiseworthy traits and the method of inculcating them. This is followed by a section that brings clarity to those matters pertaining to the thoughts of the heart, notions of the self, and the whisperings of Satan. The author does this in such a way that he simultaneously provides answers to the most common and the most specific questions people have on the issue of spirituality. Aside from this, the book provides many general and specific counsels and advices. A reader cannot but feel inspired after reading this book, and feel an immediate need to purify the heart and embellish it with praiseworthy traits.

White Thread Press is grateful to the original translator and publishers for granting us permission to edit and publish this work afresh. We have made some changes to the first edition. The language has been completely edited and revised. The Arabic terms have been left in parentheses and replaced, for ease of reading, with suitable English equivalents. Also, some portions were verified against the original Urdu text and revised where it was considered necessary, and a few sections relating to the prescription of specific daily worships and litanies were left out. We felt that these would be more appropriately acquired from a qualified representative of the Shaykh. References were added to the ḥadīths and Qur'ānic verses where missing.

An index has also been added to this edition. The biography of Shaykh Masīḥullāh Khān, which was part of the original text, has been edited and condensed for this edition and follows the main body of the book. We are very grateful to Ali Mian of Louisville, Kentucky, for compiling a brief yet sufficiently detailed biography of Ḥakīm al-Umma for this edition, providing insight into the life, piety, and academic, educational, and spiritual achievements of one of the greatest scholars of the Indian Subcontinent.

We thus present this work as *The Path to Perfection: An Edited Anthology of the Spiritual Teachings of Ḥakīm al-Umma Mawlānā Ashraf ʿAlī Thānawī.* May Allāh bless the author, his teachers, and students for their accomplishments and reward them abundantly, as well as those who assisted in the publication of this work.

Foreword

THE GREATER PART of the subject matter of this book has been extracted from various works of Ḥakīm al-Umma, Reformer of the Community (*Mujaddid al-Milla*), one who held together both the Sharīʿa and the Path (*Jamiʿ al-Sharīʿa wa 'l-Ṭarīqa*), my guide (*murshid*), Mawlānā Thānawī (Allāh be well pleased with him). Among the works from which I have extracted this material are *Al-Takashshuf ʿan muhimmāt al-taṣawwuf* (Uncovering the important issues of *taṣawwuf*), *Bawādir al-nawādir* (Unforeseen legal questions), *Qaṣd al-sabīl* (Seeking the Path), *Ḥayāt al-Muslimīn* (The life of the Muslims), *Ādāb al-shaykh wa 'l-murīd* (The etiquette of the guide and the aspirant), *Tablīgh-e Dīn* (Preaching the Religion), *Sharīʿat wa ṭarīqat* (Sharīʿa and the Path). Part of what appears in this book, I have heard personally from him while sitting in his company.

All this is in reality the abundance (*fayḍ*) and blessings (*barakāt*) of Mawlānā Thānawī (Allāh be well pleased with him), as is aptly conveyed by the following statement of Sayyid Sulaymān Nadwī (Allāh be well pleased with him): "By virtue of his teachings, spiritual training, writings, lectures, and preaching, true beliefs (*ʿaqā'id*) were spread, correct rulings (*masā'il*) were transmitted, programs for religious instruction were initiated, customs and innovations were eradicated, the Sunna of the Prophet (upon him be peace) was revived, the negligent were roused, the sleeping ones awakened, those who had forgotten remembered, those without relationships were joined to Allāh Most High, hearts kindled with the love for Allāh's Messenger (may Allāh be pleased with him), and hearts lit up with the remembrance of Allāh Most High. That branch of knowledge (*taṣawwuf*) which had become barren, once again became adorned with the treasures of the masters Shiblī, Junayd, Basṭāmī, Jīlānī, Suhrawardī, and Sarhindī (Allāh be well pleased with them)."

This attribute and rank of reformation (*tajdīd*) in this century [the twentieth] has been bestowed by Allāh Most High specifically on the Reformer of the Age: Mawlānā Ashraf ʿAlī Thānawī. May Allāh Most High perpetually shower His limitless treasures and mercies on his noble spirit, and may Allāh Most High always grant him His ranks of proximity. *Āmīn* and yet again *āmīn.*

The humble slave
MUḤAMMAD MASĪḤULLĀH
(May Allāh forgive him)

I

Taṣawwuf & the Path

All paths besides the strict
following of the Messenger of Allāh
(Allāh bless him and give
him peace) are closed to mankind.

—Junayd al-Baghdādī

Taṣawwuf

The branch of the Sharīʿa that deals with esoteric acts or states of the heart (*aʿmāl bāṭinī*) is called *Taṣawwuf*. And the branch of the Sharīʿa relating to exoteric or physical acts (*aʿmāl ẓāhirī*) is called *Fiqh*. The subject matter dealt with in *taṣawwuf* is the beautification of character (*tahdhīb al-akhlāq*), while its motive is the attainment of divine pleasure (*riḍwān*). The method of acquisition of this divine pleasure is total obedience to the commands of the Sharīʿa.

In fact, *taṣawwuf* is the spirit (*rūḥ*) and the state of perfection of the religion. Its role is to rid man's heart (*bāṭin*) of vile, unrefined attributes such as lust, anger, malice, jealousy, love of the world, love of fame, stinginess, greed, ostentation, vanity, deceit, calamities of the tongue, and the like. At the same time it seeks to adorn the heart with the lofty attributes of perseverance, gratitude, fear of Allāh, hope, abstention, unity, trust, love, truthfulness, truth, remorse, reflection, reckoning, contemplation, and so on. In this way, awareness of Allāh Most High is instilled in man. This is the true purpose of life. *Taṣawwuf* or *Ṭarīqa* does not oppose religion and Sharīʿa. On the contrary, it is obligatory upon every Muslim to become a Ṣūfī, or "one who follows the path of *taṣawwuf*." For without *taṣawwuf*, a Muslim cannot truly be described as a perfect believer.

The Need for Taṣawwuf

Now that it is clear that *taṣawwuf* is not contrary to the religion, that it is in fact a branch of the Sharīʿa, the need for it becomes obvious. Ḥakīm al-Umma Mawlānā Ashraf ʿAlī Thānawī (upon him be the mercy of Allāh) states in the introduction of *Ḥaqīqat al-Ṭarīqa:* "After rectification of beliefs and external acts, it is compulsory (*farḍ*) upon every Muslim to rectify his esoteric acts. Numerous Qur'ānic verses and an untold number of ḥadīths explicitly indicate the obligation (*farḍiyya*) of this. However, most people of superficial understanding are heedless of it because of their subservience to base desires. Who is not aware that the Qur'ān and ḥadīths are explicit regarding the significance of abstinence (*zuhd*), contentment (*qanāʿa*), modesty (*tawāḍuʿ*), sincerity (*ikhlāṣ*), patience (*ṣabr*), gratitude (*shukr*), love of Allāh (*ḥubb al-Ilāh*), contentment with the Decree (*riḍā bi 'l-qaḍā'*), trust (*tawakkul*), submission (*taslīm*), and so on, while they emphasize the attainment of these noble attributes? And who is not aware that the Qur'ān and ḥadīths condemn the opposites of these noble qualities: love for the world (*ḥubb al-dunyā*), covetousness (*ḥirs*), arrogance (*takabbur*), ostentation (*riyā'*), lust (*shahwa*), anger (*ghaḍab*), envy (*ḥasad*), and so on, and warn against them? Is there any doubt that the noble qualities have been commanded, and the base traits forbidden? This is the actual meaning of reforming the esoteric acts. This is the primary purpose of the spiritual path (*ṭarīqa*). That it is obligatory (*farḍ*) is without doubt an established fact."

In *Ṭarīq al-Qalandar,* he says, "All the authentic principles of *taṣawwuf* are found in the Qur'ān and ḥadīths. The notion that *taṣawwuf* is not in the Qur'ān is erroneous; wayward Ṣūfīs as well as superficial scholars entertain this notion. Both groups have misunderstood the Qur'ān and ḥadīths. The superficial scholars claim that *taṣawwuf* is baseless since they believe that the Qur'ān and ḥadīths are devoid of it, while the errant and extreme (*ghālī*) Ṣūfīs assert that the Qur'ān and ḥadīths contain but exoteric (*ẓāhirī*) laws. *Taṣawwuf,* they say, is the knowledge of the esoteric (*bāṭin*) and there is no need for the Qur'ān or ḥadīths (we seek refuge in Allāh). In short, both groups consider the Qur'ān and ḥadīths to be devoid of *taṣawwuf.* Thus, one group has shunned *taṣawwuf* and the other group has shunned the Qur'ān and ḥadīths altogether."

Taṣawwuf and the Qur'ān

Both external (*ẓāhirī*) and internal (*bāṭinī*) acts and duties are commanded in the Qur'ān. Allāh says in the Qur'ān, while commanding prayer and *zakāt:* "Establish the prayer and give *zakāt*" (Qur'ān 2:43), and, commanding gratitude (*shukr*), he says, "And be grateful unto Allāh" (Qur'ān 2:172). In another verse he says, "Fasting has been decreed for you" (Qur'ān 2:183), and, "Upon mankind is the pilgrimage of the House for Allāh" (Qur'ān 3:97). In another verse He says, "He (Allāh) loves them (the believers), and they love Him" (Qur'ān 5:54), and, "Those who have adopted belief are most ardent in the love of Allāh" (Qur'ān 2:165). Similarly, along with the verse "When they stand for prayer, they stand halfheartedly" (Qur'ān 4:142), is to be found "They show people" (Qur'ān 4:142), i.e., they perform prayer for ostentation (*riyā'*). The Qur'ān, just as it reprimands and condemns those heedless of prayer and *zakāt*, also mentions the evil of arrogance (*takabbur*) and vanity (*ʿujb*).

The same applies to the ḥadīths. Just as detailed chapters on prayer, fasting, trade, commerce, marriage, and divorce are to be found in ḥadīths, so too are detailed chapters on ostentation (*riyā'*), arrogance (*takabbur*), and so on found. No Muslim can deny the fact that just as the exoteric actions are divine commands, so too are the esoteric actions. "Establish the prayer and give *zakāt*" are positive commands, just as "Adopt patience" and "be grateful unto Allāh" are positive commands. As the verse "Fasting has been decreed upon you" (Qur'ān 2:183) establishes the religious nature of fasting, the verse "Those who have faith are the most ardent in the love of Allāh" (Qur'ān 2:165) establishes the religious nature of love for Allāh. On closer examination and reflection one realizes that all the exoteric actions are designed for the reformation of the esoteric actions. The purification of the heart and soul of man is the aim and the basis of salvation (*najā*) in the Hereafter, while their corruption is the cause of destruction.

Allāh Most High declares, "Verily, he who has purified the lower self (*nafs*) has triumphed, and he who has corrupted it has lost" (Qur'ān 91:9–10). And He says, "On that Day (of Judgment) neither wealth nor sons will benefit (anyone), save him who comes to Allāh with a reformed heart" (Qur'ān 26:87–89).

The first of these two verses asserts victory as being the result of the purification of the heart and soul while the second verse denies the utility of wealth and sons in the absence of a reformed heart. Belief in the articles of faith (*ʿaqāʾid*), on which hinges the acceptance of all actions, are conditions of the heart. It is clear that actions are designed for the perfection of faith. It is therefore clear that the original purpose is the reformation (*iṣlāḥ*) of the heart by virtue of which man is ushered into the Divine Court of Acceptance, and attains the lofty spiritual ranks. This is precisely what is known as *Taṣawwuf.*

Statements of the Ṣūfīs

In this regard Bāyazīd Basṭāmī (may Allāh have mercy on him) said, "Do not be deceived if you see a performer of supernatural feats flying through the air. Measure him by the standard of the Sharīʿa—how he adheres to the commands of the Sharīʿa."

Junayd al-Baghdādī (may Allāh have mercy on him) said, "All paths besides the strict following of the Messenger of Allāh (Allāh bless him and give him peace) are closed to mankind."

Abū 'l-Ḥasan Nūrī (may Allāh have mercy on him) said, "Do not venture near one who lays claim to a condition that brings about transgression of the limits of the Sharīʿa."

Khwājā Naṣīr al-Dīn Chirāgh Dehlawī (may Allāh have mercy on him) said, "Obedience to the Messenger of Allāh (Allāh bless him and give him peace) is imperative. Such obedience is essential in word, act, and intention, because love of Allāh Most High is not possible without obedience to the Messenger Muḥammad (Allāh bless him and give him peace)."

Khwājā Muʿīn al-Dīn Chishtī (may Allāh have mercy on him) said, "He who adheres to the Sharīʿa, obeys its commands, and refrains from transgression progresses in spiritual rank. All progress depends upon adherence to the Sharīʿa."

Ḥakīm al-Umma (may Allāh have mercy on him) says in *Taʿlīm al-dīn,* "Whoever acquires the wealth of arrival (*wuṣūl*: attaining the love of Allāh) has acquired it by virtue of following the Sunna."

The Technical Terms of Sharīʿa and Ṭarīqa

The source of all Islamic teaching is the Qur'ān and the Sunna. The foundation of these teachings was in the gatherings of Allāh's Messenger (Allāh bless him and give him peace), and was laid at the initial stage of Islam and existed at its main center. There were a confined number of adherents; hence, all branches of Islamic instruction—Qur'ānic exegesis (*tafsīr*), ḥadīth, jurisprudence (*fiqh*), and *taṣawwuf*—were imparted at one venue, the school (*madrasa*) of the Messenger of Allāh (Allāh bless him and give him peace). Separate departments did not exist.

However, in this school of the Messenger (Allāh bless him and give him peace) was a permanent group of lovers of Allāh and devotees of the Messenger (Allāh bless him and give him peace) who were at all times engaged in the purification of the soul and the reformation of the heart by means of practice. This group is called the People of the Ledge (*Aṣḥāb al-ṣuffa*). Later, when Islam acquired universal status, the scholars of the religion divided the sciences of Islam into separate departments. Those who rendered service to the knowledge of ḥadīth were called ḥadīth scholars (*muḥaddithūn*). Those who undertook the responsibility of Qur'ānic exegesis (*tafsīr*) were called the exegetes of the Qur'ān (*mufassirūn*). Those who specialized in jurisprudence (*fiqh*) were called the jurists (*fuqahā'*). And those who took custody of the department of purification of the heart (*iṣlāḥ al-bāṭin*) became known as the shaykhs of *taṣawwuf* or "Ṣūfīs." Hence, not a single one of the great authorities of former times ever divorced the Sharīʿa from *ṭarīqa;* on the contrary, they held *ṭarīqa* in subservience to the Sharīʿa.

Sharīʿa, Ṭarīqa, Ḥaqīqa, and Maʿrifa

The combined teachings and injunctions of Islam are known as the Sharīʿa. Both sets of acts—exoteric and esoteric—are included. In the terminology of the early authorities of Sharīʿa (*mutaqaddimūn*), the term *fiqh* (lit. profound understanding) was synonymous with the word Sharīʿa. Thus, the Greatest Imām, Abū Ḥanīfa (may Allāh have mercy on him), defined *fiqh* as "the recognition of that which is beneficial and harmful to the self (*nafs*)."

Later, in the terminology of the later authorities of Sharīʿa (*mutaʾakhkhirūn*), the word *fiqh* was used for that branch of Islam which related to exoteric acts, while the branch that dealt with esoteric acts became known as *taṣawwuf*. The ways or methods of reforming the esoteric acts are called *ṭarīqa*.

The reformation of the esoteric acts brings about spiritual radiance and light in the heart. To this heart is then revealed certain realities pertaining to tangible and intangible occurrences (*ḥaqāʾiq kawniyya*), above all virtue and vice, as well as certain realities pertaining to Divine Attributes and Acts (*ḥaqāʾiq Ilāhiyya ṣifātiyya wa fiʿliyya*), mainly affairs between Allāh and His servants. These unveilings (*makshūfāt*) are known as *ḥaqīqa*. The process of these revelations (*inkishāf*) is called gnosis (*maʿrifa*), while the one experiencing the unveiling is known as a gnostic (*ʿārif*) or *muḥaqqiq*.

All the aforementioned relates to the Sharīʿa. The notion of the Sharīʿa and *ṭarīqa* as entities apart which has gained prominence among the public is totally baseless. Now that the nature and reality of *taṣawwuf* and *sulūk* have become clear, it will be understood that unveilings (*kashf*) and miracles (*karāmāt*) are not necessary. It [*taṣawwuf*] does not promise success in worldly affairs; nor does it assert that one's work will be accomplished by means of amulets (*taʿwīdh*) and potions; nor does it claim that one will necessarily be successful in court cases by means of invocations (*duʿāʾ*). It does not promise increase in one's earnings, nor does it promise one cure from physical ailments. It does not foretell future events. It does not contend that the seeker's (*murīd*) reformation will be achieved by the spiritual focus (*tawajjuh*) of the shaykh. Extraordinary feats are not organic to *taṣawwuf*. It does not contend that the one who treads this Path will not be afflicted by the thoughts of sin, nor does it claim that the seeker will automatically (without effort) engage in worship. It does not promise total self-annihilation so that one is not aware even of one's presence. It does not promise experiences of states of ecstasy and spiritual effulgence through spiritual exercises (*dhikr* and *shughl*), nor does it claim that one will see beautiful dreams and wonderful visions.

None of the above are the aims of *taṣawwuf*. The good pleasure (*riḍwān*) of Allāh Most High is. This, then, should be kept in sight.

The Pledge

Bayʿa is a mutual pledge related to the striving for, adherence to, arrangement, and executing of the laws of exoteric actions and esoteric actions. This pledge is known as *bayʿat al-ṭarīqa,* which has been in practice through authoritative transmission from generation to generation from the earliest generations of Islam.

The Messenger of Allāh (Allāh bless him and give him peace) took pledges (*bayʿa*) from the Companions not only on *jihād,* but on Islam and adherence to the rulings of Islamic law (*aḥkām*) in general, as well as on practical deeds (*aʿmāl*). This is established by numerous ḥadīths. The following is one such ḥadīth: ʿAwf ibn Mālik al-Ashjāʿī (may Allāh be pleased with him) said, "We were with the Messenger of Allāh (Allāh bless him and give him peace), seven, eight, or nine (of us), when he said, 'Will you not give a pledge (*bayʿa*) to the Messenger of Allāh?' We extended our hands and asked, 'On what shall we make the pledge to you, O Messenger of Allāh?' He said, 'That you worship Allāh, associate nothing with Him, perform the five prayers, and that you hear and obey'" (*Muslim, Abū Dāwūd, Nasāʾī*).

On this occasion, the pledge that the Messenger of Allāh (Allāh bless him and give him peace) took from the Companions was neither the pledge of faith nor pledge to wage *jihād.* This ḥadīth is categorical evidence for the validity of the system of pledge-taking put in practice by the shaykhs of *taṣawwuf.* As there are four schools (*madhhabs*) in jurisprudence: Ḥanafī, Shāfiʿī, Mālikī, and Ḥanbalī, so too are there four schools of thought in *taṣawwuf:* the Chishtī, Qādirī, Naqshbandī, and Suhrawardī. Just as the Ḥanafī school is dominant in this area [Indian Subcontinent], the Chishtī school (of *taṣawwuf*) too is dominant here. Our elders in *taṣawwuf* give pledges in all the four orders (*salāsil*) so that respect for the four is maintained, although the Chishtī way is dominant.

The founder of the Chishtī order is our master Muʿīn al-Dīn Chishtī Ajmērī (may Allāh have mercy on him); the founder of the Qādirī order is our master Shaykh ʿAbd al-Qādir Jīlānī (may Allāh have mercy on him); the founder of the Naqshbandī order is our master Shaykh Bahāʾ al-Dīn Naqshbandī (may Allāh have mercy on him); and the founder of the Suhrawardī order is our master Shaykh Shihāb al-Dīn Suhrawardī (may Allāh have mercy on him).

The Nature of the Pledge

The meaning of *bay*ʿ, or "selling," is inherent in the word *bay*ʿ*a*, "to pledge." *Bay*ʿ*a* thus implies that the seeker (*murīd*) "sells" himself to the shaykh. In other words, he has sold himself to the shaykh in preparation for the outward rulings (*aḥkām ẓāhira*) and the inward rulings (*aḥkām bāṭina*) [to learn to give practical expression to the Law of Allāh Most High]. The nature of this "sale" envisages that the seeker of truth lay implicit trust and faith in his shaykh. He should understand and accept that the advices, prescriptions, admonitions, and prohibitions of the shaykh are all designed and motivated for his spiritual well-being. The seeker shall not interfere with or impede the diagnosis and prescriptions of the shaykh. He should have faith to such an extent that he should believe that in his knowledge there is none among creation who can benefit him more than his shaykh. In the terminology of *taṣawwuf*, this conception of implicit faith in the shaykh is known as unity of purpose (*waḥdat al-maṭlab*). Without this conception, the ceremony of pledge-taking (*bay*ʿ*a*) is meaningless and of no benefit, because congeniality (*munāsaba*) with the shaykh is an essential condition for reformation of the heart.

The sign of the existence of congeniality between the seeker and his shaykh is that the heart of the seeker does not object to the position, statements, and acts of the shaykh. Should any objection arise in the heart regarding the shaykh, the seeker should feel grief and distress.

The external form of the pledge is beneficial to the lay people (ʿ*awām*) since it induces reverence and respect in them for the shaykh. As a result, they readily accept the shaykh's statements and are constrained to act accordingly. However, for the elect (*khawāṣ*) [e.g., scholars] the pledge proves beneficial after a period has been spent in association with the shaykh. By virtue of the pledge, a bond of sincerity and association is generated between the seeker and the shaykh. The shaykh considers the seeker to belong to him and the seeker considers the shaykh to belong to him. There does not remain any tension between them.

The Mode of the Pledge

The pledge is enacted by the shaykh taking into his right hand the right hand of the seeker. If the group contracting the pledge is large, the shaykh uses a length of cloth onto which each member of the group holds with his right hand. Ladies who contract the pledge do so from behind a screen. A non-marriageable kinsman (*maḥram*) of the woman should also be present at the pledge ceremony. ʿA'īsha (Allāh be well pleased with her) says, "The Messenger of Allāh (Allāh bless him and give him peace) never touched the hand of a woman, but he would take the pledge (*bayʿa*) from her. Upon having made the pledge he would say, 'Go, for I have taken the pledge with you'" (*Bukhārī, Muslim, Abū Dāwūd*).

It is for this reason that, when entering women into the pledge, the shaykhs do so verbally, or by means of a cloth, which is spread from the shaykh to the woman behind the screen. This is the method of taking pledges when in the presence of the shaykh.

Those who are not able to present themselves personally to the shaykh can take the pledge by means of a letter or through the agency of a responsible and trustworthy person. The Messenger of Allāh (Allāh bless him and give him peace), on the occasion of *Bayʿat al-Riḍwān*, made the pledge of ʿUthmān (Allāh be well pleased with him) in his absence. On this occasion, the Messenger of Allāh (Allāh bless him and give him peace) placed his right hand upon his left hand and announced that he had made the pledge for ʿUthmān (Allāh be well pleased with him). The pledge in absence of the seeker is therefore termed the *Bayʿa ʿUthmānī* or "ʿUthmānī Pledge."

Instruction upon Taking the Pledge

Certain instructions are given to the seeker at the time of the pledge. First is the makeup and fulfillment (*qaḍā'*) of the prayers and fasts that have been missed by the seeker. The missed prayers should be made up by performing one with each one of the daily prayers of the same time. For instance, along with the Maghrib prayer of the day, a makeup of one Maghrib prayer should be made. During ʿIshā', the makeup of a missed *witr* prayer should also be made. In making up the missed prayers, only the *farḍ* and *witr* are made up. However, it is also possible to makeup a number of missed prayers collectively at one time or in a single day. In this way, the missed prayers of a person can be discharged quickly.

Second is discharging any monetary obligations. Such discharge is either by making the due payment or by obtaining the pardon of those whose rights are involved. Third is fully guarding the eyes, ears, and the tongue (from the unlawful); totally abstaining from unlawful (*ḥarām*) and doubtful (*mushtabah*) wealth; having an appearance and dress in conformity with the *sunna;* completely abstaining from innovation (*bidʿa*) and non-Islamic customs and practices on occasions of happiness and sorrow; refraining from unlawful methods in all affairs; constantly bearing in mind not to harm anyone by means of one's hand or tongue; avoiding hurting anyone; refraining from [vain] association; meeting [people] according to need; abstaining from unnecessary conversation; and constantly remembering (*dhikr*) Allāh through reciting the Pure Word (*kalima ṭayyiba*): *Lā ilāha illa 'Llāh*, "There is no god but Allāh," while walking, sitting, reclining, and lying down. The words *Muḥammad al-Rasūlu 'Llāh,* "Muḥammad is Allāh's Messenger, should be added after every few recitations.

After each prayer, recite *Āyat al-kursī* (the Throne Verse) followed by the *Tasbīḥ Fāṭimī,* which is to recite thirty-three times *Subḥāna 'Llāh,* "Transcendent is Allāh," thirty-three times *Al-ḥamdu li 'Llāh,* "All Praise is for Allāh," and thirty-four times *Allāhu akbar,* "Allāh is the Greatest."

Then, if time allows, recite the third *kalima, Subḥāna 'Llāhi wa 'l-ḥamdu li 'Llāhi wa lā ilāha illa 'Llāhu wa 'Llāhu akbar,* "Transcendent is Allāh, and all praise is for Allāh, and there is no god but Allāh, and Allāh is the Greatest," one hundred times after the Ẓuhr, Maghrib and ʿIshā' prayers.

After ʿIshā', at the time of going to bed, engage in self-reckoning (*muḥāsaba*) and contemplation of death (*murāqabat al-mawt*).

The Need for a Shaykh

It has always been in the divine scheme of things that perfection cannot be attained without an experienced instructor (*ustādh*). Thus, when one is endowed with the guidance to enter into the path, one should search for an instructor of the path, so that one may reach the true goal through the medium of this instructor's graceful guidance and excellent companionship (*ṣuḥba*).

> O my heart! If you desire to undertake this journey,
> Then hold on to the garment of the guide.
> Whoever trod the path of love without a companion
> Passed his life without attaining love.

Ḥakīm al-Umma (may Allāh have mercy on him) therefore said, "What! Has anyone attained perfection through books alone? It is simple to understand that one cannot become a carpenter without sitting in the company of a carpenter, one cannot become a tailor without being in the company of a tailor, and one cannot become a calligrapher without being in the company of a calligrapher. In short, one cannot attain perfection or become an expert in something without the companionship of an expert [in that thing]. The companionship of a pious man will induce piety in you. Similarly, the companionship of an evil man will induce evil in you. He who searches for association with Allāh Most High, has to acquire the association of the noble Friends of Allāh (*awliyā' kirām*). A short while spent in the companionship of the Friends of Allāh is more noble and superior to a century of unostentatious obedience. Companionship with the pious for even a moment is superior to a century of asceticism (*zuhd*) and obedience (*ṭā'a*)."

A Letter

The following letter from a student and reply given by Ḥakīm al-Umma (may Allāh have mercy on him) demonstrates the need for a shaykh.

> I am presently completing the *Dawrat al-ḥadīth* [ḥadīth program: the final year of Islamic education wherein the six authenticated ḥadīth collections are studied]. For quite a while I had intended to write, but a certain thing prevented me from doing so. I am a voracious reader and lover of your writings, and have been engaged in reading your books since my childhood. By the grace of Allāh, I have benefited much. I have learned one particular thing from your writings—that the commands of the Sharī'a are all voluntary (*ikhtiyāriyya*). Since the commands are volitional it follows that the commands to abstain

are likewise volitional. Thus the remedy for all spiritual ailments is to refrain (volitionally).

I have always adopted this method for myself. The question now is this: since this principle has been learned from the shaykhs of the Path, does the need still remain to refer to the shaykhs and obtain remedies from them? I do not understand this. I have ruminated for quite a while regarding this matter. I trust that you will advise me so that I may practice accordingly. After realizing this general principle, what is the need for obtaining the diagnosis and prescription of a shaykh? I hope that if I have erred, I will be informed.

The Reply

The commands and the prohibitions are all volitional. However, errors can be made in this regard. At times, what has already been acquired (*ḥāṣil*) is considered as not having been yet attained (*ghayr ḥāṣil*), and sometimes vice versa. For example, a person intends to attain concentration based on humility (*khushūʿ*) in prayer, and in reality he then attains this concentration. But, while having attained this he is simultaneously afflicted by an abundance of stray thoughts. This person then regards the accident of such thought as contradictory to concentration. He thus considers that he has not attained concentration. Furthermore, in the initial stages of , stray thoughts are non-volitional—coming of their own accord—but later on the worshipper is diverted toward volitional stray thoughts, yet he is deceived into believing that such thoughts are of the non-volitional kind of the initial stages. He thus considers himself to have concentration, while in actual fact he has lost concentration.

At times he considers what is infirm (*ghayr rāsikh*) to be firm (*rāsikh*). For example, persevering in the face of a few light mishaps, he considers himself to have attained the state of *riḍā bi 'l-qaḍā'* (satisfaction with the divine decree). His contentment in the face of these slight misfortunes leads him to believe that he has attained advanced capability in firmness and steadfastness. But when some great calamity overtakes him and he fails to be contented, he still labors under the deception that he has attained the desired degree and goal of firmness.

The consequence of regarding the attained as unattained is frustration and depression, which in turn induce one to become careless and negligent, and thus, the attained becomes truly eliminated. The harm of the opposite condition (i.e., considering the unattained as attained) is deprivation. Since one labors under the false notion that one has already achieved the goal, one does not make any effort in this direction.

The same danger lurks in considering infirm what is firm—one remains careless, not making any effort or arrangement to attain the desired goal of firmness and steadfastness. Sometimes one commits the error of believing that the state of firmness has not been attained despite its having been attained. For example, one combated unlawful lust during a time when the effect of one's *dhikr* was dominant. As a result, the condition of unlawful lust remained suppressed so much so that one's attention was totally diverted from it. Later, when the effect of the *dhikr* decreases and the natural propensities reassert themselves, even if in slight degree, one is misled to believe that one's striving against the lower self has gone wasted, hence the return of the evil propensities. The consequence of this feeling is that one loses hope and is overtaken by stagnation and retrogression.

The above are merely some examples of errors and the resultant harm. A qualified shaykh, by virtue of his insight and experience, discerns the reality of such states when informed by the seeker, and guides him aright, highlighting for him the errors and pitfalls. The seeker is thus saved from these dangers. Assuming that the spiritual traveler (*sālik*), because of intelligence and correct understanding, discerns the pitfalls himself, then too, he will not attain tranquility and peace of mind because of inexperience. He will remain perplexed. And perplexity impedes the attainment of the goal.

This is the duty of the shaykh's office. More than this is not his responsibility. Nevertheless, in kindness he performs another function as well. In realizing the goal or the initial stage of the goal or in eliminating an evil attribute, the seeker of truth undergoes great stress and difficulty although repeated subjection to such difficulty finally is transformed into ease. But the shaykh sometimes, as a favor, devises such a scheme that makes the difficulty disappear from the very inception.

This is a brief exposition for understanding. The need for a shaykh is felt and understood once one commences in the Path and systematically informs the shaykh of one's particular conditions, and at the same time follows his advice and instructions. Furthermore, such total obedience is possible only if one has full trust and confidence in the shaykh—fully resigning to him. At that time one will actually feel and realize that it is not possible to attain the goal without a shaykh.

The Signs of a Qualified Shaykh

A shaykh is one who has full knowledge and experience of spiritual ailments (*amrāḍ bāṭina*), attributes of vice and virtue (*akhlāq radhīla* and *akhlāq ḥamīda*), and their characteristics and their effects. He should further be able to distinguish between their similarities, and he must have perfect ability in devising plans and prescriptions for the acquisition of the attributes of virtue and the elimination of the attributes of vice. He has to be aware of the progress and retrogress of these attributes. He must be well versed in the hazards of the lower self and Satan, the intuitive perceptions and feelings (*khawāṭir*) pertaining to the angels (*malakūtī*) and the Divine Being (*Rabbānī*). He must be able to distinguish these various intuitive and extra-sensory feelings and perceptions. It is therefore imperative that the shaykh of the Path be one who is qualified in this knowledge and a *mujtahid* in this field, and possess natural ability and inherent propensity in it. If he has acquired the Path by a mere self-study of books on *taṣawwuf* or by listening to others, he will destroy the seeker whom he is guiding, because he will not be in a position to correctly diagnose the various states of the seeker.

Shaykh Ibn ʿArabī (may Allāh have mercy on him) briefly lists the signs of a complete and qualified shaykh (*shaykh kāmil*) as three: his *dīn* (religion) resembles the *dīn* of the messengers (upon them be peace); he prescribes [cures] as physicians; and his management and control is as that of kings.

The exposition of the above points is as follows.

1. He should possess the necessary knowledge of the *dīn,* which he must have acquired either by formal pursuit of such knowledge or from remaining in the company of firmly grounded scholars.
2. He must be a deputy (*khalīfa*) of a qualified shaykh and attached to a legitimate order (*silsila*).
3. He should be upright and pious, refraining from major sins and from continuously committing minor sins.
4. He must have derived spiritual benefit by remaining in the company

of his shaykh for an adequate period of time. Such "companionship" can either come through physically being in the shaykh's presence or through correspondence.

5. The people of knowledge (*ʿulamāʾ*) and understanding hold him in high esteem and resort to him [in matters].
6. His companionship increases one's desire for the Hereafter and divine love, and decreases one's love for the world.
7. The majority of his disciples are followers of the Sharīʿa, their conditions conforming to the demands of the Sharīʿa.
8. He is without greed and desire [for worldly gain and benefit].
9. He engages in remembrance and devotional practices.
10. He does not leave his disciples unfettered but reprimands them when the need arises, and treats everyone in accordance with respective abilities.

The one in whom these attributes exist is worthy of being a shaykh and he should be considered a wonderful alchemy. His companionship and service are in fact priceless treasures. Once these attributes and qualities are found in a shaykh, one should not be concerned about miracles (*karāmāt*) and unveilings (*kashf*). It is not necessary that these states exist in a qualified shaykh, nor is it necessary that he be one who does not earn his livelihood.

Congeniality with the Shaykh

Experience has proven that in order to gain spiritual benefit (*fuyūḍ bāṭinī*), mutual congeniality (*munāsaba*) between the shaykh and disciple is a necessary condition. Normally benefit is dependent upon affection, which is the reality of natural congeniality (*munāsaba fiṭriyya*). Sometimes a shaykh will refer a seeker to another shaykh because of the lack of such congeniality between them. In doing so the shaykh establishes, either by deduction or divine inspiration (*kashf*) that the seeker has congeniality with a certain shaykh.

In this path, it is essential that congeniality exists between the shaykh and seeker; otherwise the latter will not benefit. Such congeniality is the basis for the acquisition of benefit and passing of spiritual grace (*fayḍ*) to the disciple.

Congeniality entails that there exists between the shaykh and disciple compatibility and harmony to such a degree that the disciple discerns no rejection in his heart for any word or act of the shaykh even though the disciple may [at times] be afflicted by mental disagreement with any word or act of the shaykh. In short, harmony and compatibility are conditional for a pledge. It is therefore essential to first inculcate congeniality. This congeniality is imperative.

In the absence of this essential condition, strivings (*mujāhadāt*), certain forms of exercises designed to subdue the lower self (*riyāḍāt*), meditations (*murāqabāt*), and unveilings (*mukāshafāt*) are all futile. In the absence of natural congeniality, the disciple should endeavor to inculcate intellectual congeniality (*munāsaba ʿaqliyya*), because deriving benefit depends on it. For this reason, one should refrain from entering into the pledge until total congeniality is present.

The Benefits of the Companionship of a Qualified Shaykh

The benefits of association with a qualified shaykh are manifold. Among such benefits are that the noble and lofty qualities of the shaykh slowly pass on to the disciple. Even if the disciple is not totally reformed, he will have gained the ability to discern and recognize his faults. The disciple follows the shaykh in character and habit, attainment of joy and pleasure in remembrance and worship, enhancement of courage, and obtaining clarification and contentment from the shaykh in the event of spiritual conditions that may overcome the disciple. The disciple will discern his own spiritual conditions, which becomes manifest in the talks of the shaykh, such talks being the essence of the matter. He will increase in the desire to perform virtuous deeds. The disciple's ability in this path becomes manifest to the shaykh. Love for Allāh Most High increases. So does swift attainment of cures for spiritual ailments. He obtains the prayers (*duʿāʾ*) of the shaykh. His doubts and uncertainty are eliminated as a result of the light (*nūr*) emanating from the heart of the shaykh. This light has its effect on the disciple; spiritual darkness is dispelled by this light. The reality of all things thus becomes manifest. There are degrees regarding the efficacy of this light depending on the disposition of the seeker. One of high and noble disposition can attain the full beneficial effect of this light by merely looking at such accomplished shaykhs. In such cases the seeker attains spiritual progress and ranks without even physical association with the shaykh.

Rights of the Shaykh

The seeker should believe that he will attain his goal through the agency of his shaykh. If the seeker turns his attention elsewhere [i.e., toward another shaykh while he remains the disciple of one shaykh], he will be deprived of the spiritual grace and benefit of his shaykh. The disciple should in all ways be obedient to his shaykh and render sincere and complete service to him. In the absence of the love of the shaykh there is no real benefit. The sign of love for the shaykh is immediate fulfillment of his orders. He should never carry out any act without his permission because sometimes the shaykh resorts to an act that is appropriate for him in view of his rank and spiritual state, but the same act may be a fatal poison for the seeker.

The disciple should recite the remembrances and the litanies (*waẓā'if*) which the shaykh prescribes and refrain from all other forms of litanies. In the presence of the guide, the disciple should direct all his attention toward him. This attention has to be to such a degree that the disciple should not even perform (*nafl* "optional") prayer (in his presence) without his permission. Do not speak with anyone while in his presence; in fact, do not pay attention to anybody else. Do not stretch the legs in the direction of the guide, even if he is not directly in front of him. Never lodge any objection against the guide. If the seeker is unable to understand any act of the guide, he should not entertain any misgiving, but should recall the episode of Mūsā (peace be upon him) and Khiḍr (peace be upon him), and consider that some wisdom must lie behind the act. Never desire the guide to display miracles (*karāmāt*). When in doubt, immediately discuss the problem with the guide. Should the doubt still remain after having discussed it, consider it to be the result of your defective understanding. If the guide does not respond when the seeker puts forward his doubt, the seeker should consider that he is yet not capable of comprehending the explanation, hence the guide's silence.

He should await another opportunity for clarification. Inform the shaykh of dreams as well as any interpretation of such dreams that come to his mind. The disciple should not remain aloof from the guide without need and permission.

The disciple should not raise his voice above that of the guide nor should he speak in loud tones to the guide. When necessary, the disciple should speak to the guide clearly. He should be brief and wait attentively for the reply. He should narrate to others of the guide's advice only as much as is understandable to them. He should not narrate to others such words of the guide that they will not be able to comprehend. The disciple should not refute the words of the guide even if it seems that the disciple is correct. The disciple should hold the belief that the error of the guide is superior to the disciple's rectitude.

The disciple should inform the guide constantly of his condition, whether good or bad. The guide is the spiritual practitioner and prescribes remedies after being informed of the disciple's condition. The disciple should not maintain silence about his condition depending upon the unveilings (*kashf*) of the guide for realization [i.e., that the guide will be divinely informed] of the disciple's condition. The disciple has to systematically notify the guide of his condition. The disciple should not engage in any remembrances or litanies (*waẓā'if*) while sitting in the company of the guide. Such recitation should be in the absence of the guide.

Whatever spiritual outpouring (*fayḍ bāṭinī*) accrues, the disciple should consider it to be through the agency of the guide, even if, in a dream or state of meditation, it appears that such blessings are from a different direction [than the guide's]. If in a spiritual state, it appears that such spiritual outpouring accrued to the disciple via the agency of another shaykh, the disciple should consider that it is some manifestation of his guide, which has assumed the form of another shaykh.

Self-Reckoning

Muḥāsaba means to take stock or reckon. Here it means to take stock of one's own deeds and activities. One should reflect over the entire day's acts and deeds. Upon recalling a noble act or an act of worship, one should express gratitude unto Allāh Most High and request for greater divine guidance and success (*tawfīq*) in enhancing virtue. Upon recalling one's evil act or wrongdoing, one should become regretful. This is the daily *muḥāsaba* obligatory upon the seeker.

Contemplation of Death

This means to contemplate, to think about, the oncoming event of death. Reflect about the pangs of death, the questioning in the grave, the plain of Resurrection, the reckoning on the Day of Judgment, the presence in the Court of Allāh, crossing the Bridge (*ṣirāṭ*), and so forth. All this has to be contemplated, and a pledge is to be made that one will not venture close to sin in the future. One hundred times a day, the request for forgiveness (*istighfār*) should be made to Allāh. This can be made as follows: *Subḥana 'Llāhi wa bi ḥamdihī subḥāna 'Llāhi 'l-ʿAẓīm, Astaghfiru 'Llāha 'l-Aẓīm, Lā ilāha illā huwa 'l-Ḥayyu 'l-Qayyūm*, "Transcendent is Allāh, and all praise be to Him; transcendent is Allāh Almighty; I seek forgiveness from Allāh Almighty; there is no god but He, the Living, the Self-Subsisting."

Consider yourself to be most inferior, so much so that if you observe with your own eyes another indulging in the worst of vices, then too you shall not despise that person, nor shall you consider yourself nobler than him. On the contrary, one should fear and bear in mind that it is very possible that the perpetrator of the vice may resort to sincere repentance (*tawba*) and become a person of high piety, while the one who despised the sinner may become ensnared (Allāh forbid) in the meshes of the lower self and Satan and be diverted from worship and obedience. One has no certainty regarding one's end. Therefore, one has no basis for regarding another with contempt.

This is the first step in seeking (*sulūk*). Without taking this step, the path of *taṣawwuf* remains closed.

The Spiritual Struggle

Allāh says:

> Those who strive in Our cause, We will most assuredly guide them in Our ways (Qur'ān 29:69).

Fuḍalā' al-Kāmil narrates that the Messenger of Allāh (may Allāh bless him and give him peace) said:

> The *mujāhid* is he who strives (*jihād*) in the obedience of Allāh (*Bayhāqī*).

The reality of spiritual struggle (*mujāhada*) consists in the habitual practice of opposing the lower self (*nafs*). In other words, it is to check and control the physical, pecuniary, egotistical, and mundane desires, delights, and preferences of the lower self in the pursuit of obedience and the good pleasure of Allāh Most High. Two types of benefits accrue to the lower self: *ḥuqūq* (rights or obligations) are such benefits necessary for the endurance and existence of the physical body and life; and *ḥuẓūẓ* (pleasures, delights, luxuries) are benefits in excess of the rights.

Mujāhada and *riyāḍa* [abstinence—forms of austere exercises designed to establish the control of the spirit over the lower self] are directed toward the luxuries. In spiritual struggle, reduction or total abstention from the pleasures and luxuries are advocated. [Pleasures here refer to lawful pleasures and not to such pleasures which are forbidden in the Sharīʿa.] In the employment of spiritual struggle, the rights and obligations are not destroyed, for such destruction is contrary to the Sunna. The noble ḥadīth states: "Verily, your self (*nafs*) has a right over you." Destruction of the rights brings about physical weakness and the health deteriorates. When this happens, one finds it difficult to execute even the necessary duties and acts of worship.

The Need for Spiritual Struggle

Righteous works (*aʿmāl ṣāliḥa*) are always accompanied by labor, toil, and difficulty because such works are in conflict with the desires of the lower self. There will always be some form of opposition—sometimes great, sometimes slight—by the lower self against righteous works. Striving against the self is therefore a life-long process.

Both the spiritual beginner (*mubtadī*) and the adept (*muntahī*) are at times faced with lethargy because of conflict in the righteous works. Both need to ward off their lethargy by means of spiritual struggle. However, the beginner stands in greater need of spiritual struggle. In the initial stages, he at times becomes overconfident. But frequently, natural traits and habits return, and the consequence is an urge to sin. Thus, the lower self of the adept also at times becomes lethargic in obedience. He therefore stands in need of spiritual struggle at such a time.

There is, however, a great difference between the spiritual struggle of the beginner and the adept. The beginner is like one who is seated on the back of a horse just trained. The rider of the newly trained horse has to be much more alert and exercise greater control over the horse, as such a horse tends to be more wild and apt to go out of control. The adept is like a rider seated on the back of a well-trained horse. He exercises no great endeavor to keep the horse under control. Nevertheless, he too has to be alert because even a trained horse sometimes reverts to wildness because of its natural animal traits. But the slightest warning from the rider is sufficient to check the horse. If, however, the rider is totally negligent, then even the trained horse will sometimes suddenly drop him from its back. Hence, spiritual struggle for the control over the lower self is necessary for the adept also.

Moderation in Spiritual Struggle

The purpose of spiritual struggle is not to depress and frustrate the lower self, but to habituate the lower self to effort, and to eliminate the habit of comfort and luxury. For this purpose that amount of spiritual struggle is sufficient which brings some difficulty to bear upon the lower self. It is of no benefit to impose excessive strain on the lower self and frustrate it. Excessive strain will render it useless. Understand this well. Effort and trial are not always meritorious. It is desirable if in moderation, and resulting in beneficial progress. Excess in spiritual struggle is contemptible; hence, observance of moderation is a must. Shaykh Saʿdī (may Allāh have mercy on him) echoes this in the couplet:

> Eat not so much that it spills from the mouth;
> Eat not so little that the body is overcome with weakness.

Allāh Most High says in the Noble Qur'ān: "[The servants of Allāh are] those who, when they spend, do not waste nor become miserly. But between these [extremes of waste and miserliness] they are moderate" (Qur'ān 25:67). Moderation is therefore to be observed in spiritual struggle; but this moderation should not be prescribed according to one's own opinion and desire. The degree of moderation and the method of struggle should be taken from a spiritual master (*muḥaqqiq*).

Types of Spiritual Struggle

There are two types of spiritual struggle. Physical: this is the imposition of practices upon the lower self in order to accustom it to difficulties; for example, accustoming the lower self to prayer by imposing upon it supererogatory prayers in abundance, or reducing the greed of the lower self by means of abundance of supererogatory fasts. Opposition: in this type of struggle the lower self is opposed in its desires. When the lower self urges one to commit a sin, opposition is offered. The main type of spiritual struggle is the second kind; it is compulsory (*wājib*). The first type is employed in order to attain the second kind. When the lower self becomes accustomed to difficulties it will develop the habit of controlling its desires.

Those who possess the ability to control their desires without resorting to physical struggle [the second] are not in need of this [first] type of struggle. However, because such people are extremely few, the Ṣūfīs have stringently adopted physical struggle as well. According to the Ṣūfīs physical spiritual struggle consists of four fundamentals (*arkān*):

1. *Qillat al-ṭaʿām:* eating less,
2. *Qillat al-kalām:* talking less,
3. *Qillat al-manām:* sleeping less,
4. *Qillat al-ikhtilāṭ maʿa 'l-anām:* associating less with people.

One, who fully acquires these four qualities and becomes accustomed to observe them, will attain the ability to control his lower self. He will be in a strong position to check the evil desires of the lower self.

Spiritual struggle against the lower self in its urge to sin is acquired when the lower self is opposed to a certain degree, even in its lawful desires: refusal to fulfill immediately the desire of the lower self for some delicious food, its urge for such food being rebutted and only fulfilled after vehement desire so that the lower self does not become frustrated. When one becomes accustomed to oppose the lower self in things lawful (*mubāḥāt*), then it will become relatively simple to oppose the sinful urges of the lower self. A person who grants his lower self absolute freedom in lawful things will at times not be able to suppress the urge for sinning.

Overview

Spiritual exercises (*riyāḍa*) and spiritual struggle (*mujāhada*) have two fundamentals (*arkān*): *mujāhada ijmālī* or *mujāhada jismānī* (physical struggle); and *mujāhada nafsānī* (opposing the lower self) or *mujāhada tafṣīlī* (mental opposition).

Physical struggle has the four fundamentals stated above. In these acts [reduction of food, speech, sleep, and association] it is necessary to adopt moderation in accordance with the instruction of a qualified shaykh. Neither is there to be excessive indulgence in these acts, because the result will be indolence and negligence, nor should there be excessive reduction, for the consequence will be physical weakness.

Mental opposition is divided into two classes: *akhlāq ḥamīda,* beautiful and praiseworthy character traits, and *akhlāq radhīla,* repulsive and blameworthy character traits.

Exposition of the Four Fundamentals of Spiritual Struggle

1. Talking Less

Allāh Most High says:

> He utters not a word but that a vigilant guardian is at hand (Qur'ān 50:18).

The Messenger of Allāh (Allāh bless him and give him peace) said:

> He who maintains silence has attained salvation (*Aḥmad, Tirmidhī*).

The Prophet ʿĪsā son of Maryam (peace be upon them) said:

> Do not speak in abundance other than with the remembrance of Allāh, for your hearts will become hard. Verily, a hard heart is far from Allāh, but you know not. And do not look at the sins of people as if you are the overseers. Gaze at your sins as if you are slaves. People are of two kinds: the one who is involved (in sin) and the one who is saved (from sin). Have mercy upon those involved and praise Allāh Most High for protection (received) (*Mālik*).

Abundance of speech hardens the heart, eliminating thereby humility and reverent fear [of Allāh]. This fact is established by experience. A person becomes distanced from Allāh Most High because of the hardness in the heart, but one fails to realize this drift from Allāh Most High. The reality of it will be discerned in the Hereafter. Although the effects of such distance from Allāh are detectable here as well, due to lack of concern one fails to realize this. One should not view the sins of others as if one has been appointed over others; on the contrary, one should be concerned with one's own sins, so that reparation can be offered and rectification adopted. Some people are involved in sin and others again have been protected from sin.

One should have mercy upon those who have become involved in sin and not despise or criticize them. Admonish them with kindness and supplicate on their behalf. Protection against sins is a safeguard; hence, one should not be vain and arrogant if one is saved from sin. Rather, one should consider such protection as a favor from Allāh, a favor to which one is not entitled, and be grateful.

Further explanation

Man's conversation apparently falls into three categories: the beneficial, i.e., such speech that has some worldly or religious benefit; the harmful, i.e., such speech that has some worldly or religious harm; and that which is neither beneficial nor harmful. The ḥadīth describes this third category of speech as *lā yaʿnī* (nonsensical, useless). On closer examination it will be realized that this third class of speech belongs also to the second category—harmful talk. If *Subḥāna 'Llāh* were uttered once during a time squandered in useless talk, then half the pan in the Scale of Deeds would be filled. If some advantageous or righteous act were done during the time spent in futile conversation, it would become an expiation for sin and a medium of salvation in the Hereafter. If not this, then at least such time idly spent could be expended in some worldly benefit. The Messenger of Allāh (Allāh bless him and give him peace) said, "A sign of one's Islam being healthy is one's [shunning of that which does not concern him, i.e.,] shunning futile acts and futile talks" (*Tirmidhī*).

In [Ghazālī's] *Iḥyā' ʿulūm al-dīn,* it is mentioned that a reckoning will be made (in the Hereafter) of *lā yaʿnī* (futile) speech. There is therefore no certainty that one will be saved from something that will be submitted to reckoning. The struggle to reduce conversation is more difficult than the struggle to reduce food and sleep. In eating, preparation to a certain extent is involved. Moreover, there is a limit to food consumption. Indigestion due to excessive eating will by itself compel one to reduce eating. Similarly, there is a limit to sleeping.

On the other hand, conversation requires no effort, and no difficulty is experienced in keeping the tongue in operation. Man resorts to pleasures so as to experience delight and joy. Conversation aside, enjoyment of all pleasures (*ḥuẓūẓ*) diminishes with increased indulgence. Eating with a full stomach does not bring about any enjoyment of the food. Excessive sleep, too, is not enjoyable. But the enjoyment derived from speaking is limitless. In fact, pleasure increases the more one speaks. Hence, reducing conversation is the most difficult. In spite of this difficulty, freedom in it (i.e., speech) has not been granted because of the evils involved in excessive speech. One becomes greatly involved in sin because of speaking much. Reducing speech has therefore been stipulated as a fundamental of spiritual struggle.

Reducing speech does not mean reduction in such talk that is necessary. It means shunning nonsensical or useless conversation, even if such talk happens to be lawful. If this habit is inculcated, then abstention from unlawful speech, such as falsehood, scandalizing, slander, and so on, will be automatic. Abstaining from unlawful discussion comes within the scope of true spiritual struggle—struggle that is obligatory. If one becomes accustomed to refrain from idle talk (although it may be lawful), which falls within the scope of secondary struggle, then to a far greater degree will one practice true spiritual struggle (compulsory striving against unlawful talk). It is not permissible to shun talk that is necessary, since this will result in problems or cause inconvenience and difficulty to the audience.

Explanation of Necessary

"Necessary" here means a need that, if refrained from, will result in harm. Therefore, if by refraining from a certain conversation the result is some worldly or religious harm, such talk will be necessary. An example of necessary talk is the conversation that a trader has with customers in order to promote his sales. As long as his talk is in the interests of his trade, it is regarded as necessary. Refraining from such talk will result in worldly loss; hence, the Sharīʿa gives permission for such an exchange. Necessary conversation of this kind has absolutely no detrimental effect on the heart. The heart does not darken the slightest bit by necessary talk. The illustrious gnostics have found that even a full day spent in necessary talk will not adversely affect the heart. An auctioneer can spend the entire day in selling by means of talking, but such talk will not darken the heart one iota because such talk is necessary. On the other hand, a single statement spoken unnecessarily will darken the heart.

The Sharīʿa's prescription for reducing speech does not mean sealing the mouth, but it envisages that the tongue be kept occupied with the recitation of the Majestic Qur'ān or with remembrance of Allāh Most High. In this way the struggle to reduce speech will be most beneficial. By means of this struggle, the tongue remains detached from sin; the habit of nonsensical discussion is reduced (or eliminated), and along with it limitless spiritual rewards are obtained. By constantly engaging the tongue in remembrance such benefits are reaped, which are unobtainable by maintaining silence.

The Remedy

Prior to speaking, ponder for a few moments. Endeavor to understand whether Allāh Most High, who is the Hearing and the Seeing, will be pleased or displeased with what you are about to say. If this method of contemplation is adopted before speaking, and then the lower self urges one to indulge in sinful or nonsensical talk, confront it with courage and suppress the urge. If any unbecoming words were spoken then compensate immediately for it by repenting. If the talk involved abuse or mockery of anyone or scandalizing gossip about anyone, then after repenting, seek the pardon of the person concerned as well.

If for some reason it is difficult to obtain the necessary pardon (e.g., the person concerned may be away or may have died) then seek Allāh's forgiveness for the person concerned as well as for oneself. Such forgiveness could be asked in the following way: "O Allāh forgive us and forgive him."

Our master, Shaykh Farīd al-Dīn ʿAṭṭār (may Allāh have mercy on him) explained most beautifully, perfectly, and comprehensively the benefits of maintaining silence. He said, "Nothing nobler than silence enters my mind. Silence contains so many benefits that they cannot be explained. Silence makes breasts the treasure house of pearls of wisdom. I learned this hidden secret from the oyster's shell."

A drop of water enclosed in the oyster's shell is transformed into a pearl. Similarly, man's breast becomes a treasure house for pearls of wisdom by means of closing his lips.

2. EATING LESS

Allāh Most High says:

> Eat and drink, but do not waste. Verily, He does not love those who transgress the limits (Qur'ān 7:31).

The Messenger of Allāh (Allāh bless him and give him peace) said:

> *Tasbīḥ* and *taqdīs,* which suffice the people of heaven, will suffice them too (*Mishkāt al-Maṣābīḥ*), i.e., the believers.

This ḥadīth shows that, as *tasbīḥ* (glorifying Allāh) and *taqdīs* (hallowing Allāh) suffice for the Angels in the heavens, so will it suffice as nourishment for Muslims. It is narrated that certain saints remained without food for long periods in solitude engaged in glorification and hallowing. It is clear from this ḥadīth that at times, remembrance and glorification are sufficient as nourishment.

However, it is not possible to adhere to the methods of food reduction practiced in former times. The people of those days were endowed with great physical strength, and despite the great reduction in food consumption they suffered no ill effect and maintained full concentration in their acts of worship. Their physical strength could be gauged from the type of spiritual exercises they practiced. Some of their practices were of such a severe nature that if anyone attempted to practice them today, he would break his back. An example is *ṣalāt al-maʿkūs* (upside down prayer), which consists of one suspending oneself upside down and in this inverted manner carrying out some exercise.

In reality, the Messenger of Allāh (Allāh bless him and give him peace) did not prescribe reduction in food, but altered the routine times of eating and in this way made the intervals between eating times longer. This change of habit (in eating times) and the longer intervals (between them) which are difficult upon the lower self, have been considered by the Sharīʿa to be representative of reduction in food. Among the various forms of struggle, fasting is the best. Hence, the Sharīʿa has given reduction in eating the form of fasting. The other forms of reduction in food adopted by the people of spiritual struggle have no original basis in the Sharīʿa. Eating meagre amounts and remaining hungry are not forms of struggle of the Sharīʿa. The significance (*faḍīla*) of hunger mentioned in ḥadīth does not refer to self-imposed hunger, but refers to involuntary hunger—hunger that comes one's way uninvited. The ḥadīth consoles such impoverished persons by explaining the virtues of hunger so that they do not worry and suffer unduly.

Patience in the face of such divinely imposed hunger occasions reward and elevation in spiritual ranks. The significance of hunger is similar to the significance of illness explained in the ḥadīth. The ḥadīth even mentions reward for illness, but this does not mean that one should voluntarily induce illness. The method of reduction in food mentioned in the book *Tablīgh al-dīn* [*Al-Arbaʿīn*], by Imām Ghazālī (may Allāh have mercy on him) has been forbidden because reduction in food is not the intended purpose of the Sharīʿa, and because the physique of people today is unlike that of the people of earlier times.

Reduction in food is not an end in itself, but a means of acquiring a specific aim. This aim is to weaken the animal urge in man, and thereby prevent the lower self from sinning. Therefore, if the self can be controlled and restrained from sin without reducing food then reduction in eating is not necessary. Furthermore, cheerfulness and joy in worship are experienced if the body is in the state of health and strength. Experience shows that nowadays health, in most cases, suffers as a result of reduction in food. At the same time, one must abstain from excessive eating and adhere to moderation. The capacity of people differs; hence, moderation will differ for different persons. The guideline in this matter is to eat when hungry and to stop eating when you feel that you can still eat a few more morsels. In other words, one is allowed to eat to one's fill, but not to satisfy one's craving.

3. SLEEPING LESS

Allāh Most High says:

> Stand up during the night, but a portion (of the night); half the night or less than half the night (Qur'ān 73:2–3).

This verse commands standing up during the night so that the lower self becomes accustomed to striving. In this way the ability of the lower self (to submit to righteousness) is strengthened and perfected. Standing up during the night is most efficacious for bringing the lower self to submission. All forms of worship, be they supplication, recitation, prayer, or remembrance, be they external (*ẓāhir*) or internal (*bāṭin*), are fulfilled in the proper manner during the night. The meaning of proper external performance of acts of worship during the night is the proper and correct recital of the words since the time available is ample. The meaning of proper internal performance of acts of worship is that during the night one derives greater pleasure in worship. This is in fact what the tongue and the heart conforming means.

The Sharīʿa has ordered the performance of *Tarāwīḥ* prayer during the night in the month of Ramaḍān because it envisages reduction of sleep. As fasting has its role in reducing food, the *Tarāwīḥ* prayer has its role in reducing sleep. As the change of habit [in eating times] during fasting induces *mujāhada*, so too does the change of habit in *Tarāwīḥ*. The general habit prevailing is to sleep after ʿIshā'. The command of *Tarāwīḥ* brings about a change in the habit of sleeping, and this changing of habit is difficult on the lower self. This is precisely spiritual struggle.

In reducing sleep, the Sharīʿa does not stop at mere wakefulness, but instructs the observance of acts of worship during the time of wakefulness. Allāh praises pious servants in the Qur'ān: "In the middle of the night they ask for forgiveness" (Qur'ān 51:18). Elsewhere in the Qur'ān it is said, "They separate their sides from the beds calling on their Lord in fear and hope" (Qur'ān 32:16). In other words, they perform the prayer during the night.

The trend of the verse is inclusive of all forms of worship; hence, it applies to supplication and remembrance as well. Furthermore, aside from the religious benefits of sleeping less, one's physical health also benefits. Less sleep creates a light (*nūr*) on the face. The following is the statement of a ḥadīth scholar with regard to this: "The face of one who performs prayer in abundance during the night becomes beautiful during the day." Excessive sleep is detrimental to the physical health as well. It reduces or stunts the capacity of contemplation in a person. This in turn brings about harm in both religious and worldly activities. A person given to excessive sleeping is never punctual.

Moderation in Reducing Sleep

Moderation in this struggle is also desirable. Nowadays this moderation means sleeping at least six or seven hours. If sleep becomes overpowering one should not ward it off. In this case postpone your act of worship and sleep. The act of worship should be completed later. If the sleep is not over-powering then one should adopt courage and remain awake. If sleep is warded off when it is really over-powering the consequence will be harmful to the mind as well as to the body. Confused thoughts will arise in the mind, and at times one can be deceived into believing such confused thoughts to be inspiration (*ilhām*). Such a person might consider himself to be a saint. The final result would be insanity. Hence, the Messenger of Allāh (Allāh bless him and give him peace) said, "When any of you rises in the night and finds that he is unable to recite the Qur'ān properly (due to drowsiness), and he does not know what he is reciting, he should lie down" (*Muslim*).

The advice in such cases of sleepiness is to lie down and not to ward off sleep. Some people who are extreme in their observance of reducing sleep and other aspects of spiritual struggle, and do not comprehend the possibility of harm, should heed this ḥadīth. It is an admonishment for them.

The advice given in this ḥadīth is twofold. At times extremism in spiritual struggle proves detrimental to the physique. When the words are not recited correctly because of overpowering sleep then the necessary rewards will not be obtained. Thus remaining awake will serve no beneficial purpose.

4. ASSOCIATING LESS WITH PEOPLE

Unnecessary association with people should not be increased. Remember that besides Allāh, there are three kinds of association. Praiseworthy association: the Sharīʿa commands, for in itself it is association with Allāh Most High. Ending such association is not permissible. Blameworthy association: the Sharīʿa prohibits. Ending such association is compulsory (*wājib*). Permissible association: this is neither worship nor sin. It is not necessary to end such association. Although permissible, there is a need to reduce such association. The instruction to discontinue association refers to detestable and permissible association and not praiseworthy association. Yet, insofar as blameworthy association is concerned, the discontinuance must be total: such association is to be compulsorily ended. As for permissible association the meaning is reduction or limiting such association.

As long as the relationship with the Creator is not well established and grounded, association with the creation is extremely harmful. The ostensible reason advanced for association with people—meeting their obligations—can be truly fulfilled only if the relationship with the Creator is firmly grounded. If the relationship with Allāh has not been firmly established, then neither is the duty to creation fulfilled, nor the duty to the Creator. This fact has been proven by the experience of thousands of Friends (*awliyāʾ*) of Allāh.

Solitude is permissible. In fact, best for one who has no worldly or religious duty, pertaining to himself or others, to discharge. Such solitude is of greater merit during times of strife and mischief when it becomes difficult to have patience in the face of anxiety, agitation, confusion, and anarchy. The ḥadīths have extolled solitude during such circumstances. The Messenger of Allāh (Allāh bless him and give him peace) said in this regard, "[...] and a man who takes to solitude on the peak of a mountain with his goats whose rights he fulfills and he worships Allāh" (*Tirmidhī*).

In another ḥadīth it is said that: "Soon a time will dawn when the best form of wealth for a Muslim will be goats. He will go with them to a peak of a mountain and to places where rainwater accumulates. He will flee from mischief taking his religion with him" (*Bukhārī*).

Solitude [i.e., total dissociation from people] is not permissible for one with duties and obligations to discharge, whether they pertain to others or oneself, and whether it be personal obligations: providing maintenance to one's family when one does not have the ability of *tawakkul* (trust in Allāh), or religious obligations: the acquisition of necessary religious knowledge. Certain ḥadīths that prohibit solitude refer to these two states just mentioned. Such an example of prohibition is the case of our master ʿUthmān ibn Maẓʿūn (Allāh be well pleased with him). He was forbidden from adopting solitude since he was still in need of gaining knowledge of the religion. At the same time, Muslims also were in need of him regarding matters of the religion, especially in the fields of propagation and development of Islam.

The above explanation pertains to solitude that is permanently adopted. However, temporary solitude for a few days is necessary for the beginner in most cases.

The Benefits of Solitude

Among the numerous benefits of solitude is the abstention from sin provided that in solitude control is exercised over the eyes. The ears as well as the heart have to be guarded in solitude. The thought of anyone besides Allāh Most High should not deliberately be brought to mind. In the event of any such stray thought entering the mind, the one sitting in solitude should immediately ward off the thought by engaging in remembrance of Allāh. In such well-guarded solitude, there is indeed great protection against sin. It is quite manifest that prevention against evil has priority over the acquisition of some gain; hence solitude has priority over association. Although associating [with others] has many benefits, many sins follow in its wake nevertheless. Furthermore, reducing conversation is difficult in association. Only the *ṣiddiqūn* and spiritual masters are able to exercise perfect control over their tongues [as well as other emotions] even in association with others. In most cases, useless and nonsensical discussions take place when one associates with others. The hearts of those who have no solitude in their time become progressively stripped of spiritual effulgences.

The Benefits of Association

For certain persons, in particular circumstances, association is beneficial. Among such benefits are acquisition of knowledge (*taʿallum*) and imparting knowledge (*taʿlīm*). *Taʿlīm* and *taʿallum* are dependent upon association. Association affords the opportunity of rendering service to creation. The significance and benefits of group prayer is available by means of association. One who has adopted total solitude is deprived of the rewards of group prayer and service to creation. Humility is also a result of association. The spiritual magnificence of the religion is obtained by means of associating with the Friends of Allāh.

The Effective Method

Carry out every act and duty at its stipulated time. Worldly duties in their time and worship in its time. Even occasional humor and lighthearted talk to cheer the hearts of Muslims should be resorted to at opportune times. One's daily life should be conducted in this controlled manner. Total solitude is not always ideal, for at times zeal and enthusiasm in one are dulled, and it then becomes difficult to progress.

Service to creation is extremely beneficial for the traveler (*sālik*), but his association should not exceed the time required for rendering his service to creation. Association in excess to the required measure is fraught with spiritual evils and harm. One should not increase one's association and connections, for such increase interferes with remembrance of Allāh.

One should remain in solitude as long as the heart finds solace in, and unity with Allāh Most High. However, when one becomes disturbed and frustrated in solitude as a result of a multitude of thoughts striking the mind, one should withdraw from solitude and sit in company. But it is essential that the company be pious. Stray thoughts and frustration will be eliminated in such company. In such circumstances association is like unto solitude.

These four matters—the reduction of speech, of food, of sleep, and of association with people—belong to the physical forms of spiritual struggle. In the ensuing pages the mental forms of spiritual struggle will be discussed.

Character Traits

Khalq and *khulq* are two different terms. *Khalq* refers to external form, whereas *khulq* means the internal dimension. Man, while consisting of body and physical parts, also consists of spiritual forms: spirit (*rūḥ*) and lower self or ego (*nafs*). His physical body has been given the faculty of sight (*baṣāra*), which is exercised by the eyes of the body. Similarly, he has been given the faculty of insight or seeing with the eyes of the heart (*baṣīra*). The external eyes lack the ability to perceive the internal dimension.

Allāh Most High has created man with these two component parts in different moulds. He has bestowed them with different physical forms along with various internal forms. Some have a beautiful form and character and some have ugly form and character. The physical form is known as *ṣūra,* while the spiritual or internal form is known as *sīra.* The rank of *sīra* is higher than that of *ṣūra* because Allāh Most High has related the former to Himself. In this regard He says, "I blew in him [Ādam] My spirit (*rūḥ*)" (Qur'ān 15:29).

In this verse, Allāh relates *rūḥ* to Himself. In another verse, He says, "Say, the *rūḥ* is of the Command of my Lord" (Qur'ān 17:85). This indicates that the spirit is not lowly nor of dust. However, Allāh Most High relates the physical body to soil. He says, "Verily, I shall create man from soil" (Qur'ān 38:71). The meaning of "spirit" in this context is the substance, which was generated by the direct inspiration of Allāh Most High. Each such substance acquires cognition of things in proportion to its inherent ability.

It has thus been established that the object of greater honor and importance is the command of Allāh: the *sīra* of man. As long as beauty is not inculcated into the internal dimension of man, he will not be described as having a beautiful *sīra.* Allāh Most High has granted the physical body limbs: hands, feet, and so forth. Similarly has He bestowed "limbs" to the internal form. The "limbs" of the internal form are the faculties of knowledge, wrath, desire, and justice. A *sīra* cannot be called beautiful until these four faculties have been adorned. Imperfection in the *sīra* is comparable to deformity in the physical body (*ṣūra*). As a deformed physical body cannot be called beautiful, neither can a defective internal form. For example, if one's faculty of anger (*quwwa ghaḍabiyya*) is below the level of equilibrium and one's faculty of desire (*quwwa shahwāniyya*) is excessive, one's character (*sīra*) cannot be called beautiful.

Equilibrium and Beauty of the Four Internal Faculties

1. THE FACULTY OF KNOWLEDGE

Equilibrium (*iʿtidāl*) of knowledge is man's ability to distinguish between statements of wrong and right, between beliefs of falsehood and truth, and between deeds of vice and virtue. When this ability has been cultivated, the fruits of wisdom (*ḥikma*) will be experienced. Regarding such wisdom, Allāh Most High says, "He who has been granted wisdom has indeed been granted abundant good" (Qur'ān 2:269). In reality, this wisdom is the root of all merits and excellence.

About Intelligence

Equilibrium in intelligence (*ʿaql*) makes man wise, cultured, sharp-witted, and farsighted. His advice will be sound and he will possess the ability to act correctly in all affairs. Ingenuity manifests in him. If intelligence exceeds equilibrium it will be called deceptive and fraudulent. Intelligence below the degree of equilibrium is ignorance, dim-wittedness, and stupidity. The consequence is that such a person is easily misled. In short, man is described as having a beautiful *sīra* only when all these faculties are in the state of equilibrium. It has been said that the best of affairs is its middle (its state of equilibrium). Allāh Most High says, "Our servants are such that when they spend they neither are extravagant, nor are they miserly, but they remain in a condition in between [in the state of equilibrium]" (Qur'ān 25:67).

Internal beauty (*sīra*) varies with people just as external beauty (*ṣūra*) differs. The possessor of the most beautiful *sīra* was the Messenger of Allāh (Allāh bless him and give him peace). About his excellence, Allāh declares, "Verily, you are of splendid character" (Qur'ān 68:4).

Among the Muslims, the degree of beauty of character (*sīra*) will be in proportion to the degree to which they resemble the character of the Messenger of Allāh (Allāh bless him and give him peace). The greater their resemblance to the character of the Messenger of Allāh (Allāh bless him and give him peace), the greater the beauty of their *sīra*. It is evident that success and fortune in the Hereafter will be in proportion to the beauty of *sīra* acquired.

2 & 3. THE FACULTY OF WRATH & THE FACULTY OF DESIRE

Equilibrium of these two faculties is that both operate along the lines of wisdom and Sharīʿa, submitting in entirety to the demands and commands of the Sharīʿa and upholding its prohibitions.

The faculties of wrath and desire should be like the trained hunting dogs of a hunter or like a well-trained horse, answering and acting in accordance with the call of the master. When these conditions are cultivated and become praiseworthy, man will be described as the repository of beautiful character. His *sīra* is said to be beautiful.

About the Faculty of Wrath

When this faculty is in the state of equilibrium it is known as valor (*shujāʿa*). This is praiseworthy to Allāh Most High. An excess in this faculty is called recklessness (*tahawwur*), and a deficiency is called cowardice (*jubn*). Both recklessness and cowardice are reprehensible.

In the wake of the laudable state of valor flow the qualities of kindness, chivalry, courage, generosity, forbearance, steadfastness, tenderness, ability to restrain anger, dignity, and farsightedness in all affairs. The state of recklessness produces inexperience, boastfulness, pride, inability to restrain anger, and vanity. The state of cowardice creates fear, disgrace, contempt, and inferiority. All these lowly qualities find external manifestation.

About the Faculty of Desire

Equilibrium of the faculty of desire is called chastity (*ʿiffa*). When this faculty exceeds equilibrium, it is termed greed (*ḥirṣ*) and lust (*hawā*). Allāh Most High loves the condition of chastity. The excellent traits produced by chastity are generosity, shame, patience, contentment, and *taqwā*. In this state man's covetousness (*ṭamaʿ*) decreases, fear and humility increase, and the wish to aid others is engendered. If this faculty falls below equilibrium, it results in greed, expectation, flattery, servitude to wealthy persons, contempt for the poor, shamelessness, extravagance, show, narrow-mindedness, impotence, envy, and so forth.

4. THE FACULTY OF JUSTICE

Equilibrium of the faculty of justice is to hold the reins of the faculty of wrath and the faculty of desire and to ensure that they conform to the religion and intelligence. Intelligence is like the king, and justice is like the vizier. It has to comply with the orders of the king.

All Character Traits are Natural

All the *sīra's* character traits are natural propensities. Insofar as natural propensity is concerned, an attribute is neither blameworthy nor praiseworthy. The attributes become praiseworthy or blameworthy through operation. The Messenger of Allāh (Allāh bless him and give him peace) said, "He who gives for the sake of Allāh and withholds for the sake of Allāh, verily, he has perfected his faith" (*Abū Dāwūd*).

The stipulation "for the sake of Allāh" is related to both "giving" and "withholding." It is clear from this that unrestricted generosity is not praiseworthy, nor is economy [i.e., to withhold spending] in itself reprehensible. Both are praiseworthy if employed for the sake of Allāh Most High, and both are reprehensible if not for the sake of Allāh Most High.

The principle governing the elimination of blameworthy character traits is "for the sake of Allāh" or "not for the sake of Allāh." Allāh willing, this will be explained in detail below. All reprehensible attributes are interrelated. Therefore, the lower self will only come under one's control after the elimination of all such traits. Rectifying one trait while ignoring another will not prove beneficial. One afflicted by a number of diseases will be considered healthy only after all the diseases have been cured. Similarly, man will have acquired a beautiful internal form when all his internal conditions have become praiseworthy. The Messenger of Allāh (Allāh bless him and give him peace) said that a Muslim is he whose character is perfect. He also said that the noblest believer is one who has the best character. This basis is thus called religion, and the Messenger of Allāh (Allāh bless him and give him peace) came to perfect this religion (*Aḥmad*).

Types of Character Traits

There are two types of internal character traits (*akhlāq bāṭinīyya*). One type is related to the heart and the other to the lower self. Internal character traits pertaining to the heart are called the praiseworthy character traits (*akhlāq ḥamīda*) and the properties of excellence (*malakāt fāḍila*). These are also referred to as stations (*maqāmāt*). They consist of: *tawḥīd* (unity of actions—that nothing happens without the will of Allāh), *ikhlāṣ* (sincerity), *tawba* (repentance), *maḥabba Ilāhī* (love of Allāh), *zuhd* (abstinence), *tawakkul* (trust in Allāh), *qanāʿa* (restraint), *ḥilm* (forbearance), *ṣabr* (patience), *shukr* (gratitude), *ṣidq* (truthfulness), *tafwīḍ* (consignment of one's affairs to Allāh), *taslīm* (submission), *riḍā* (contentment with the Decree), *fanā'* (annihilation), and *fanā' al-fanā'* (annihilation of annihilation).

The type of internal character traits pertaining to the lower self are called blameworthy character traits (*akhlāq radhīla*). They are *ḥirṣ* (greed), *ṭamaʿ* (covetousness), *ṭūl al-amal* (prolonged vain hopes), *ghaḍab* (rage), *kidhb* (lying), *ghība* (backbiting), *ḥasad* (envy), *bukhl* (avarice), *riyā'* (ostentation), *ʿujb* (vanity), *kibr* (arrogance), *ḥiqd* (malice), *ḥubb al-māl* (love of wealth), *ḥubb al-jāh* (love of fame), and *ḥubb al-dunyā* (love of the world).

The process of purifying the self of these attributes is called *tazkiyat al-nafs*. With regard to this, Allāh Most High says, "He who has purified his self, verily, he has attained success" (Qur'ān 87:14).

II

Blameworthy Character Traits

Do not venture
near one who lays claim
to a condition that
brings about transgression
of the limits of the Sharīʿa.

—*Abū 'l-Ḥasan Nūrī*

Greed

Allāh Most High says:

> Do not raise your eyes toward the glitter of the worldly life that We have granted to various groups among them (the unbelievers) (Qur'ān 15:88).

The Messenger of Allāh (Allāh bless him and give him peace) said:

> The son of Adam ages, while two things in him grow younger: greed for [more] wealth and greed for [more] life (*Bukhārī, Muslim*).

The Nature of Greed

The heart's obsession with wealth is greed (*ḥirṣ*). Greed is the root of all spiritual ailments. It is, therefore, proper to describe it as the mother of all maladies. All mischief and strife are the consequences of this base attribute. It is because of greed that people plunder and usurp the rights of others. The basis of immorality is the lust for bestial pleasure. The root of all blameworthy character traits is this very greed.

All the gnostics maintain that the foundation of blameworthy character traits is arrogance (*kibr*), and arrogance is like the craving for fame. Thus, the basis of arrogance too is greed.

If man possesses two valleys filled with gold and silver, by nature he will desire a third. The more the demands of greed are satisfied, the greater will its demands be. The greedy person is like one afflicted by a rash. The more he scratches, the worse the rash becomes. Allāh Most High says, "What! Is there for man everything he desires?" (Qur'ān 53:24)

In other words, it is not possible for man to fulfill all his desires. It is for this reason that the greedy have no peace of mind. Nothing besides soil [that is, the grave] can satiate his greed. Before a wish is fulfilled, another develops. When one is not contented with destiny, one is smitten by a multitude of desires and hopes whose fulfillment is most difficult. The result of non-fulfillment of desire is frustration and worry. The greedy, in spite of perhaps possessing abundant wealth and enjoying luxury, are perpetually afflicted with frustration.

The Remedy

Reduce expenditure. This will lessen concern with and desire for more earnings. Forget about the future and bear in mind that the greedy are ever loathsome.

Covetousness

Allāh Most High says:

> Follow not caprice, for it will lead you astray [away from the Path of Allāh] (Qur'ān 38:26).

The Messenger of Allāh (Allāh bless him and give him peace) said:

> A weakling is one who follows his desire and then has hopes [of compensation from] Allāh (*Tirmidhī*).

The Nature of Covetousness

Covetousness (*ṭamaʿ*) means a preference for things that conflict with the Sharīʿa. The highest degree of such desire is unbelief and associating others with Allāh. The lowest degree is distraction from perfect obedience. Straying from the Straight Path is common to all forms of covetousness.

The Remedy

The remedy for covetousness is spiritual struggle—to accustom oneself to oppose the desires of the lower self so that the carnal and material cravings of the lower self are subordinated to the pleasure of Allāh Most High. Spiritual struggle is to restrain the demands of the lower self, whether such restraint is simple or difficult.

Anger

Allāh Most High says:

> And those who swallow anger and those who forgive people, Allāh loves the righteous (Qur'ān 3:134).

The Messenger of Allāh (Allāh bless him and give him peace) said:

> Do not become angry (*Bukhārī*).

and

> A strong man is not one who defeats (another) in physical combat. Verily, a strong man is he who controls his self at the time of anger (*Bukhārī, Muslim*).

In another narration it is said that a strong man is he who controls anger. It is essential to keep anger under control. One should never act spontaneously in accordance with the dictates of anger. On the contrary, anger should be made subservient to the commands of the Sharīʿa. It is natural to be aroused in the state of anger. Such natural propensity is not blameworthy [in itself]. But Allāh Most High has endowed man with willpower. Anger has therefore to be controlled since it is within the scope of man's willpower to do so. Failure to exercise this volitional power is contrary to human nature.

There are many reasons for the inclusion of anger in the natural attributes of man. Along with the quality of anger, Allāh Most High has endowed man with the ability to control such anger to ensure that it is not misdirected and unjustly employed. Anger in itself arises involuntarily. It is automatically activated. But acting in accordance with its demand is voluntary; hence, refraining from it is likewise voluntary. The remedy for a non-volitional act (the way of curbing it) is nothing other than the exercise of one's willpower in order to bring about restraint and control. This is within one's ability even if one experiences a degree of difficulty in exercising willpower. Repeated exercise of the will weakens the demands of anger. In consequence, refraining from anger becomes a relatively simple task.

The following narration appears in the noble ḥadīth: "A judge should not decide between two parties while angry" (*Bukhārī, Abū Dāwūd*). The judge or the ruler is not permitted to issue a verdict while angry, but should postpone the trial for a later date. The term *judge* in the context of this ḥadīth applies to every person with authority over people. The instructor, teacher, and head of a family all fall within the scope of this ḥadīth. They should not hasten to mete out punishment upon their subordinates while angry.

Those in authority should remember that Allāh Most High is the defender of the rights of those who have no defender. Allāh Most High will demand from the aggressor the rights of the oppressed. According to the noble ḥadīth, Allāh Most High and the Messenger of Allāh (Allāh bless him and give him peace) will claim from the tyrannical ruler the rights he usurped even from his non-Muslim subjects. It is therefore imperative to exercise caution when passing judgment.

In cases of injustice carried out in the state of anger, it is essential that the aggressor, after his anger has subsided, publicly apologize and humble himself in the presence of the one whom he has wronged. The aggressor should personally apologize in profusion and seek the pardon of the one he wronged. This measure will restore the anger of the aggressor to equilibrium. He will thus be prevented from the perpetration of injustice at the behest of anger.

At all times, avoid haste. Strive seriously to oppose the dictates of anger. Whenever you succumb, resort to asking for forgiveness and obtain the pardon of the one whose rights have been violated. Recite: *Aʿūdhu bi 'Llāhi mina 'sh-Shayṭāni 'r-rajīm,* "I seek refuge in Allāh from Satan the accursed."

When overcome by anger, sit down if you happen to be standing, lay down if sitting. Perform ablution with cold water or drink cold water. Divert your attention by immediately engaging in some other activity, especially reading, which is very effective in curbing anger. If all this fails to eliminate anger, withdraw from the presence of the one who is the object of your anger.

Remember that Allāh Most High has greater power and authority over you and that you are disobedient to Him. If He adopts the attitude of wrath toward you, where will you be then? Also reflect that nothing can happen without the will of Allāh. Ponder then, of what worth am I? I am an absolute nonentity. How can I then act in conflict with Allāh Most High?

Falsehood

Allāh Most High says:

> Refrain from false statements (Qur'ān 22:30).

The Messenger of Allāh (Allāh bless him and give him peace) said:

> Make truth obligatory upon you and beware of falsehood (*Bukhārī, Muslim*).

The Nature of Falsehood

Falsehood (*kidhb*) is to speak contrary to fact. For a person to be considered a liar, it suffices that he report every rumor without investigating whether it is a fact or not. The Messenger of Allāh (Allāh bless him and give him peace) ordered abstention from lies because falsehood and immorality are complementary partners and both will be in Hellfire. The Prophet (Allāh bless him and give him peace) said that giving false evidence three times is like *shirk*.

In a vision, the Messenger of Allāh (Allāh bless him and give him peace) was shown a man whose cheeks were being repeatedly slit from ear to throat. The cheeks would heal immediately upon having been slit, and the process would be repeated. Upon inquiring, the Messenger of Allāh (Allāh bless him and give him peace) was informed by Jibrīl (peace be upon him) that the one being punished was a liar and that the punishment would continue [in the grave] until Resurrection (*Bukhārī*).

In another ḥadīth, it is related that a woman called her child. To entice the child into coming to her, she indicated to the child that if he came, she would give him something. The Messenger of Allāh (Allāh bless him and give him peace) asked her what she would give him if the child came? She replied that she would give dates. The Messenger of Allāh (Allāh bless him and give him peace) then commented that if she had no intention of giving the child anything, her statement merely being to lure the child to her, then such a statement would also be a lie (*Abū Dāwūd*).

The Remedy

When speaking, be cautious. Do not speak without thinking. Think before you speak, and be firm in confronting and curbing the urge to speak what is false. If falsehood is spoken, make up for this error by seeking forgiveness. Should any word contrary to the Sharīʿa pass your lips, resort to repentance in profusion.

Envy

Allāh Most High says:

> Say! I seek refuge with the Lord of the morning ... from the evil of the envier when he envies (Qur'ān 113:1,5).

The Messenger of Allāh (Allāh bless him and give him peace) said:

> Do not envy each other (*Bukhārī*).

The Nature of Envy

To be displeased with another's good position and to wish for its elimination is envy (*ḥasad*). Envy has three stages: the natural human quality—in this degree of envy, man is excused and is not at fault; acting according to the demands of envy—in this degree, man is a sinner; opposing the demands of envy—in this degree, man is laudable and will be rewarded.

Generally, the basis of envy is pride (*takabbur*) and deceit (*ghurūr*). Without any valid reason man seeks to withhold the bounties of Allāh Most High. He desires [at times consciously and at times subconsciously] that just as he withholds from giving to others, Allāh too should withhold His bounties from others. Envy is a disease of the heart. It is harmful to both one's spiritual life and worldly life. The harm to man's religion (spiritual life) consists in the eradication of his good deeds, and he becomes the victim of Allāh's Wrath. The Messenger of Allāh (Allāh bless him and give him peace) said, "Envy devours good deeds as fire devours wood" (*Abū Dāwūd*).

The harm to his worldly life consists in frustration and worry, which perpetually afflicts the envious person. He is consumed by frustration caused by envy for another whose disgrace and fall he always anticipates. In this way the envious destroys his Hereafter in addition to destroying his worldly comfort and peace of mind.

The Remedy

Envy is remedied by praising much the person against whom envy is directed. Praise him no matter how difficult this may seem. Honor him and meet him with respect and humility.

Miserliness

Allāh Most High says:

> He who is miserly is in fact miserly only to himself (Qur'ān 47:38).

The Messenger of Allāh (Allāh bless him and give him peace) said:

> The miser is far from Allah, far from Paradise, far from people, and close to the Fire (*Tirmidhī*).

The Nature of Miserliness

Miserliness (*bukhl*) is to withhold spending when such spending is necessary according to the Sharīʿa and in order to be generous. Miserliness has two stages: what is contrary to the command of the Sharīʿa—this stage is sinful; and what is contrary to kindness (*muruwwa*)—this degree of miserliness, although not sinful, is not good. Elimination of even this degree of miserliness is commendable and meritorious.

According to the noble ḥadīth, wealth spent to protect one's honor is also charity (*ṣadaqa*). Miserliness is a severe malady, so the Messenger of Allāh (Allāh bless him and give him peace) exhorted, "Save yourself from miserliness, for it has destroyed nations before you" (*Muslim*).

It is not, therefore, befitting for a Muslim to be miserly. In being miserly one is paving the path to Hellfire. Miserliness in reality is the effect of love for wealth, which directs man's attention to the world. The consequence of this is the weakening of the bond of love with Allāh Most High. At the time of death the miser looks on his wealth with regret and sorrow. He has to embark on his journey into the Hereafter reluctantly and forcibly because, in him, there is no desire to meet Allāh Most High. According to the ḥadīth, the one who at death has no desire to meet Allāh Most High is of the people of Hellfire.

The Remedy

Constant remembrance of death expels the love of wealth from the heart.

Ostentation

Allāh Most High says:

> They display to people [their acts of worship] (Qur'ān 4:142).

The Messenger of Allāh (Allāh bless him and give him peace) said:

> Verily, even a little ostentation is *shirk* (*Ibn Māja*).

The Nature of Ostentation

Ostentation (*riyā'*) is the intention to enhance one's dignity in the eyes of people by means of acts of obedience to Allāh Most High. This attitude totally defeats the purpose of worship. The purpose of worship is to gain the pleasure of Allāh Most High. Since show or display of worship involves division of purpose, ostentation is termed the lesser *shirk* (*shirk aṣghar*). By means of ostentation one splits the purpose of worship by endeavoring to attain both public acclaim as well as the pleasure of Allāh Most High. In this regard Allāh says in the Noble Qur'ān, "He who hopes for the meeting with His Lord should practice righteousness and associate none with the worship of his Lord" (Qur'ān 18:110). The exegetes have explained that the meaning of "and associate none in the worship of his Lord" is "to refrain from ostentation."

Qāḍī Thanā'ullāh [Pānīpatī, the great exegete of the Qur'ān] explained this verse as follows: "He (the worshipper) does not exhibit his good acts nor does he seek reward or praise for his virtuous deeds from anyone besides Allāh Most High" (*Tafsīr Maẓharī*).

It is also mentioned in the noble ḥadīth that on the Day of Resurrection, when Allāh Most High compensates people for their deeds, the people of ostentation will be commanded to go to those they did their works for and ask them for reward (*Tirmidhī, Aḥmad*). In a lengthy ḥadīth, it is said that on the Day of Resurrection three persons will be ushered into the presence of Allāh Most High. These three will be a scholar, a generous person, and a warrior who had waged *jihād*. These three will proffer their respective acts of worship to Allāh Most High, who will say to them, "You performed these deeds in ostentation and for acclaim. You committed these acts so that people would say, 'You are a great scholar, a generous person, and a great warrior.' You have already gained what you sought. People have already praised you on earth. You have therefore no right here. Enter the Fire" (*Muslim*).

The Messenger of Allāh (Allāh bless him and give him peace) also said that a deed contaminated by even an atom of ostentation is unacceptable to Allāh Most High (*Marāsīl Qāsim ibn Mukhaymir*). Heed this and reflect! In view of the above, never intend to display any act nor intend to conceal it. Concern yourself with the act itself, intending thereby only the pleasure of Allāh Most High. Ignore all diversionary stray thoughts and whisperings of the lower self and the devil that enter your mind. You may at times be assaulted by the thought that your act is to obtain the acclaim of the people. Ignore this whispering, which in fact is a ploy of the devil or the lower self engineered to sidetrack you from performing the righteous act. Prior to performing a good deed, reflect and ascertain your motive. What is your intention for doing the act? Is it to seek the pleasure of Allāh Most High or the pleasure of others? If you discern any of the contamination in your intention, then purify your intention. Rid it of the contamination and firmly resolve to perform the deed for the pleasure of Allāh Most High.

The Remedy

The cure for ostentation is to rid the heart of the desire for fame and name. Ostentation in fact is a branch of *ḥubb al-jāh* (love of fame and glory). Perform your acts of worship in solitude. This worship in solitude refers to worship that does not have to be performed in a group (*jamāʿa*). However, regarding congregational prayer, the elimination of love of fame is enough to combat ostentation. Another efficacious remedy against ostentation developing in an act of worship is to perform that specific act of worship in abundance. Within a short while the ostentation will be dispelled, and by force of habit the worship will become sincere.

Vanity

Allāh Most High says:

> [Remember] when your great number pleased you [instilling vanity in you] (Qur'ān 9:25).

The Messenger of Allāh (Allāh bless him and give him peace) said:

> And the destroyers are desires followed, miserliness obeyed, and a man being pleased with himself, and [of the things that destroy] this [last] is the worst of them (*Bayhaqī*).

The Nature of Vanity

Vanity (*ʿujb*) is to attribute one's excellence to oneself while being oblivious of the possibility of such excellence being snatched away by Allāh Most High. Vanity is a cloaked and subtle trick of the lower self, which always desires to occupy a distinguished rank (above others). The lower self finds pleasure in this desire. Allāh Most High detests anyone who considers himself distinguished, laudable, and the vessel of excellence.

Delight over the bounties granted by Allāh Most High is not vanity. Such true delight is not unrestricted and does not produce vanity, since the fear of the elimination of the bounties is ever present in the heart. One realizes that the excellence or bounty that one has gained is purely a gift from Allāh Most High, who has awarded it because of some act or knowledge [which is also the favor of Allāh], and one further realizes that Allāh Most High has the full power to take away the bounty at any time He desires. This experience of delight is therefore not vanity. On the other hand, a person suffering from vanity becomes neglectful and fails to see that the bounty in his possession is in fact a gift from Allāh Most High. One afflicted with vanity thinks himself entitled to the bounties.

Vanity resembles pride in all aspects, save one; vanity does not necessarily require that others be one's inferiors. A person suffering from vanity considers himself to be of a lofty rank without necessarily regarding another to be his inferior. According to the noble ḥadīth, on the Day of Resurrection, the man of vanity, strutting about in overconfidence, will meet Allāh Most High, and He will be irate (*Aḥmad*).

The Remedy

Always regard excellence and virtues that one possesses to be the gifts of Allāh Most High. Contemplate the power of Allāh and fear the possibility of the gifts being taken away. Consider your faults, both internal and external, so that the idea of perfection and self-righteousness is abolished.

Pride

Allāh Most High says:

> Verily, He does not love the proud (Qur'ān 16:23).

The Messenger of Allāh (Allāh bless him and give him peace) said:

> He who has a grain of pride in his heart will not enter Paradise (*Muslim*).

The Nature of Pride

Pride (*takabbur*) is to consider oneself superior to others in attributes of excellence. There are many forms of pride. Most are subtle, hidden, and hard to detect. It is only the thorough gaze of a qualified shaykh that can uncover such hidden forms of pride. In this matter, even the scholars who concern themselves with only the external rulings of the Sharīʿa (*ʿulamā' al-ẓāhir*) are constrained to follow an expert in the path of *taṣawwuf.* In a nutshell, pride is to willingly and consciously regard oneself superior to others in religious or worldly excellence in a way which creates contempt in the heart for others. This is the reality of pride, and this is forbidden. Pride consists of two ingredients: the feeling of superiority and considering oneself great, and contempt for others.

Pride not willingly advanced, but entering the heart against your will, is not sinful. Such non-volitional pride is merely the external dimension or form of pride. Up to this stage pride is not sinful. But when one willingly entertains the feeling of pride, which initially crept in against one's will, it is sinful pride. In th is case, the mere form of pride is transformed into the reality of pride.

Where the condition of contempt for others is non-existent, pride will not arise. Mere belief in superiority and inferiority, prominence and insignificance, is not pride. For example, an older person considering an infant to be younger than him without the notion of contempt for it is not pride. But the one who consciously thinks himself better than others becomes arrogant. His lower self swells up with pride, the consequences of which manifest themselves. Examples of pride are: to regard others with contempt, to take offence when others do not greet one first, to feel insulted if others do not offer one respect, to be annoyed when someone admonishes one, refusal to concede the truth even after having realized it. May Allāh Most High keep us under His protection and save us from pride, for indeed, it is the severest of maladies. It is the root of all spiritual ailments.

It was pride that made the devil a deviant. The noble ḥadīths therefore sound dire warnings with regard to pride. Allāh Most High has warned that the abode of the proud ones will indeed be terrible (Qur'ān 40:76). Pride is the exclusive prerogative of Allāh Most High. Allāh Most High will destroy all those who desire to participate in this exclusive attribute of greatness (*Mustadrak*). The Messenger of Allāh (Allāh bless him and give him peace) said that the proud will be encased in trunks of fire in Hell.

The Remedy

This malady is remedied by reflecting on the splendor, glory, and majesty of Allāh Most High. This reflection will produce in one a realization of one's own humble position. Your own excellence will then fade into nothingness. Also, humble yourself in the presence of those whom you regard as your inferiors. Be respectful to them so that you become filled with humility.

Malice

Allāh Most High says:

> Be forgiving, command righteousness, and sever yourselves from the ignorant ones (Qur'ān 7:199).

The Messenger of Allāh (Allāh bless him and give him peace) said:

> Do not feel malice toward one another (*Bukhārī, Muslim*).

The Nature of Malice

This is the condition of malice (*ḥiqd*) that asserts itself in the state of anger when one lacks the power to take revenge. It is the seed of many evils. When anger has not been satisfied, its vapors engulf the heart, producing a seething effect that boils the heart. This vapor and sentiment plants the malice in the heart. This results in frustration. Malice is an intentional condition. It is not the feeling of mere dislike, which arises against your will. In malice, one entertains evil in the heart for another by design, and at the same time one is busy with schemes to harm the one at whom the malice is directed. If intention and desire to harm are absent, it will not be malice, but will be known as dejection (*inqibāḍ*), which is not a sinful state as this is a natural condition.

The Messenger of Allāh (Allāh bless him and give him peace) said that "two persons harboring malice for one another are not forgiven" (*Muslim*). The reference to this malice is malice based on injustice and wrong. Hatred for the sake of religion is not within the scope of the malice described here. Such hatred is meritorious, since the ḥadīths command that love be for the sake of Allāh and hatred for the sake of Allāh (*Aḥmad*).

The Remedy

The cure for malice is to overlook the fault of the one toward whom malice is felt and to associate with him irrespective of the difficulty one may experience in the adoption of such a kindhearted attitude.

Love of Fame

Allāh Most High says:

> As for that abode of the Hereafter, We reserve it for those who do not desire greatness on earth nor [do they desire] corruption. And ultimate triumph is for the pious (Qur'ān 28:83).

The Messenger of Allāh (Allāh bless him and give him peace) said:

> Two hungry wolves let loose in a flock of sheep do not cause as much harm as the harm to a man's religion wrought by his desire for wealth and fame (*Tirmidhī*).

The Nature of the Love of Fame

The desire that others honor, respect, and be submissive to one is termed love of fame (*ḥubb al-jāh*). It is difficult to diagnose this malady. It is only in the event of an incident in which one is not honored that this disease becomes detectable. Love of fame is a quality that lies in one's imagination; hence, its nature is transitory. It is extremely flimsy in that it is dependent on the thoughts of others, for fame entails honor of one by others. The thoughts of others thus form the basis of fame. If others divert their thoughts, one's fame is eliminated. Hence, he who desires to be considered famous and honorable has to rely on the thoughts of others—thoughts that are not within his control. But in spite of love of fame being so flimsy in nature and ephemeral, man hankers after it.

Only such fame is detestable that has been acquired by one's desire and pursuit. Such fame is a calamity that destroys one's worldly life as well as one's life of the Hereafter. When man sees that the world praises him, he is overtaken by pride and vanity. These diseases finally destroy him. His religion is thus destroyed. Many people have fallen into this trap and been utterly wiped out.

A famous person has many envious enemies who engage in conspiracies to harm and eliminate him. This then is the harm to one's worldly life. Thus, both religion and worldly life suffer in the wake of fame.

On the other hand, fame that Allāh Most High bestows upon man without him requesting it is a bounty (*niʿma*). As man needs wealth to a certain degree, so does he stand in need of fame to a certain degree. Such limited fame enables him to remain in safety and be protected against injustice and oppression. Such safety enables him to engage in the worship of Allāh Most High without fear and in peace. This amount of fame is therefore not harmful.

The Remedy

Meditate upon the futility of love of fame. Neither the one who honors nor the one who is honored will remain. All will perish. It is therefore childish to be delighted over such a transitory and illusionary attribute. This manner of contemplation will eliminate this malady.

Love of the World

Allāh Most High says:

> The worldly life is nothing but the comfort of illusion (Qur'ān 3:185).

The Messenger of Allāh (Allāh bless him and give him peace) said:

> The world is the prison of the believer and the paradise of the unbeliever (*Muslim*).

The Nature of Love of the World

All things that give pleasure here to the lower self without being of any merit in the Hereafter are termed *dunyā* (the world). We are afflicted with a number of spiritual ailments all having their origin in the love of the world. About this disease, love of the world (*ḥubb al-dunyā*), the Messenger of Allāh (Allāh bless him and give him peace) said, "Love of the world is the root of all evil" (*Bayhaqī*).

If this root ailment is treated and cured, all other maladies flowing from it will also disappear. A man overwhelmed by love of the world has no concern and time for the Hereafter. Such a person without care for the Hereafter will not be bothered about righteous deeds nor will he abstain from evil. The one in whom there is love of the world has very little concern for the religion. Increase in the degree of love of the world brings about a corresponding decrease in concern for the religion. Utter love of the world entails an utter lack of concern for the religion. This is manifest in the unbelievers.

The world does not mean wealth and family. The world is the intentional and voluntary adoption of anything evil that causes one to become forgetful of Allāh Most High irrespective of what that thing might be. Thus, acquisition of wealth and other material means is not evil; love for such material objects is evil. Wealth is like the water in the ocean, and the heart of man is like the ship sailing on the ocean. Water, while it facilitates the movement of the ship, can also sink it. As long as the water remains outside the ship, it aids its sailing. But entry of the water into the ship causes it to sink. Similar is the case of wealth. Wealth aids man as long as it remains outside his heart. However, if its love enters the heart it will bring about his destruction.

A noble ḥadīth states, "Lawful riches are a benefit to a pious man" (*Aḥmad*). He benefits because he spends his wealth in meritorious ways. On the contrary, if love of wealth takes hold of the heart of man, he curbs the rights of others. When the treasures of the Persian empire were ushered into the presence of our master ʿUmar (Allāh be well pleased with him), he recited the Qur'ānic verse, "The love of pleasures has been made beautiful to mankind" (Qur'ān 3:14). He then commented, "O Allāh! It is evident that the desire for pleasure is inherent in us. Its total elimination is not the aim. But we supplicate that wealth aids us in the attainment of Your love."

The world under critique is like a serpent whose skin is colorful and most beautiful, but whose poison is fatal. Intelligent people maintain a distance from such danger and are not lured by the externally adorned skin. But a little child unaware of the danger of a snake is attracted by the external beauty and is prepared to grab hold of the snake. We are like the little child. We are attracted to the world by its external beauty and adornment without being aware of its dangers. Men of intelligence and experience do not incline toward the world.

People are generally deceived and overwhelmed by the glitter of the world because they are not aware of its reality. Should the reality of the world be revealed, they would become utterly disillusioned and detest it. A noble ḥadīth states, "If the value of the world were equal to that of the wing of a mosquito, in the eyes of Allāh, He would not have allowed any unbeliever even a drink of water from it" (*Tirmidhī, Ibn Māja, Aḥmad*).

In the eyes of Allāh Most High the world has no value. It is a detestable object. He therefore prefers it for His enemies. A man aware of the realities is fearful of an object detested by Allāh Most High. The Messenger of Allāh (Allāh bless him and give him peace) described the world in the following similitude: "What relationship with the world have I? My likeness is as a traveler on a mount, halting in the shade of a tree (for a short) while, only to leave it again and proceed along the way" (*Tirmidhī, Ibn Māja, Aḥmad*). The traveler rests a while in the shade and then moves on again.

The Remedy

Remember death often and do not involve yourself in farfetched hopes. The pursuit of distant schemes and material enterprises should be shunned. In this way, the love of the world will be eliminated from the heart.

This elimination is in fact the stage at the end of the Path [which the seeker travels in his spiritual journey]. In fact, one has to become imbued with the spirit and quality spoken of in the following: "Die before your death" [an aphorism of the Ṣūfīs that at times is incorrectly attributed to Allāh's Messenger (Allāh bless him and give him peace)]. This means that one has to inculcate the attribute of the dead in oneself even before death, and that attribute is the lack of love of the world.

III

Praiseworthy Character Traits

He who adheres to the
Sharīʿa, obeys its commands,
and refrains from transgression,
progresses in spiritual rank:
all progress depends upon
adherence to the Sharīʿa.

—Khwājā Muʿīn al-Dīn Chishtī

Unity

Allāh Most High says:

> And Allāh has created you and your deeds (Qur'ān 37:96)

and

> And you desire nothing, but that Allāh desires it (Qur'ān 81:29).

The Messenger of Allāh (Allāh bless him and give him peace) said:

> Know that if all creation united to benefit you, they would not be able to grant you any benefit but that which Allāh has ordained for you. And if they united to harm you, they would not harm you in the least but that which Allāh has ordained for you (*Tirmidhī, Aḥmad*).

The Nature of Unity

Unity (*tawḥīd*) in this discussion refers to *tawḥīd afʿālī* or "unity of actions." This means that one must have implicit and strong faith in the fact that without the Will of Allāh nothing can happen. This state of unity is acquired by contemplating the weakness of creation and the power of the Creator.

Sincerity

Allāh Most High says:

> They have not been commanded but to render [their] worship unto Allāh, sincerely establishing the religion for Him and turning away from all others (Qur'ān 98:5).

The Messenger of Allāh (Allāh bless him and give him peace) said:

> Verily, Allāh does not look at your external forms and your wealth, but He looks at your intentions and actions (*Muslim*).

The Nature of Sincerity

Sincerity (*ikhlāṣ*) means to intend Allāh in one's acts of obedience. The motive must only be the proximity and good pleasure of Allāh Most High. This motive must not be contaminated by personal motives of gain or the pleasure of others.

Acquiring Sincerity

Elimination of ostentation is precisely the acquisition of sincerity.

The Benefits of Sincerity

No matter how righteous and no matter how trivial an act may be, if it is accompanied by sincerity, it will be permeated with *baraka* (blessing). Rewards will increase in proportion to the degree of sincerity. For this very reason has it come to us in a ḥadīth: "Half a measure (*mudd*) [of corn] given in charity by my Companions is nobler than gold equal to Mount Uhud given in charity by others" (*Bukhārī, Muslim*). The secret is the degree of sincerity. The sincerity of the Companions is far superior to the sincerity of others. Their reward is in terms of their sincerity and love.

The highest stage of sincerity is the rendering of an act for the sake of Allāh Most High alone, creation having absolutely no connection in one's motive. A lesser degree of sincerity is that the act is rendered to please people but not motivated by any desire for worldly gain. The motive is merely to please others. The third degree of sincerity is to render an act without having any motive. The motive is neither the religion nor the world. This too is sincerity: it is the absence of ostentation.

Repentance

Allāh Most High says:

> O believers! Make repentance unto Allāh Most High, a pure repentance (Qur'ān 66:8).

The Messenger of Allāh (Allāh bless him and give him peace) said:

> O people! Make repentance unto Allāh (*Muslim*).

The Nature of Repentance

Repentance (*tawba*) is the regret and sadness that arises in the heart when remembering a sin. For the validity of the repentance, shunning the sin, firmly resolving to abstain from it in future, and controlling the lower self when it calls for the sin are necessary.

The meaning of repentance is to return from distance to proximity. It has a beginning and an end. The beginning of repentance is the diffusion of the rays of the Light of Gnosis (*nūr al-maʿrifa*) in the heart, which then realizes that the sin committed is a fatal poison that wreaks spiritual disaster. This realization induces regret and fear, which result in a true and sincere yearning to compensate for the sin. This yearning is of such a degree that shunning the sin is immediate. Further, a firm resolve and intention are made to totally abstain from the sin in future. Along with this intention a full effort is made to compensate for past shortcomings. When the result is this fruit of repentance pertaining to the past, present, and future, then perfection of repentance has been acquired. This then is the end of repentance.

The Need for Repentance

It should be clear that repentance is compulsory (*wājib*) upon every person because Allāh Most High addresses all Muslims in the verse, "O believers! Make repentance unto Allāh, a pure repentance" (Qur'ān 66:8).

Since the reality of repentance is to regard sin as a fatal poison and disaster for the life of the Hereafter, and to firmly resolve to shun sin, this much of repentance is part of faith. Its being compulsory and necessary is apparent to every believer. Hence, Allāh Most High says, "He who makes repentance after his transgression and reforms, verily Allāh turns toward him" (Qur'ān 5:39).

The meaning of this verse is that Allāh Most High will forgive, have mercy upon, and aid the person, who after having sinned, renders repentance according to the dictates of the Sharīʿa and reforms his acts for the future—he abstains from all evil, practices in conformity with the Sharīʿa, and remains firm in his repentance.

How to Make Repentance

Repentance is to confess to Allāh Most High one's sins and to regret committing them. It is the firm resolve to discharge all the rights of others and other duties that are obligatory, but which have not been rendered. This intention should be made immediately, and thereafter the actual fulfillment of such rights and duties should be put into motion. Alternatively, the pardon of those whose rights were usurped should be obtained. When a sin has been committed, immediately perform two *rakʿas* of prayer with the intention of repentance. One then has to offer repentance with both the tongue and heart. The repentance should be made fervently and vigorously. If one is unable to shed tears, then one's face should take on the appearance of a concerned and crying person while making repentance.

For the purpose of making repentance, recall your sins and then offer repentance in profusion. However, do not reflect upon the sins committed nor make vigorous attempts to remember what sins had been committed, for this attitude will create a barrier between the one repenting and Allāh Most High. This constitutes an obstacle on the path of love and progress. After having made sincere repentance, if previous sins come to mind, then renew the repentance. Do not be overly concerned about sins for which repentance has already been made.

While making repentance, there should be a degree of moderation in mentioning the sins. There is no need to recite a whole list of sins while making repentance. Seek forgiveness for all sins in general. According to a ḥadīth one should say, "And I repent of even sins that You are more aware of" (*Muslim*), and, "I repent of sins that I am aware of and sins that I am unaware of" (*Aḥmad, Mustadrak*).

Pondering sins is a waste of time and a diversion from the remembrance of Allāh. However, one should make special repentance for sins that one recalls automatically. The real goal is Allāh Most High and not the remembrance of sins, nor the remembrance of acts of obedience. The purpose of remembering sins is to offer repentance. Hence, once repentance has been made, one should not deliberately and consciously ponder sins, thereby making such remembrance a definite purpose, because this will engender the idea that Allāh Most High is displeased with one, and this is a dangerous idea.

Acquiring Repentance

Remember and reflect upon the warnings sounded in the Qur'ān and ḥadīth with regard to sins. The pang of regret that enters the heart as a result of such reflection is repentance.

Love of Allāh

Allāh Most High says:

> He [Most High] loves them and they love Him (Qur'ān 5:54)

and

> Those who have faith are strongest in love for Allāh (Qur'ān 2:165).

The Messenger of Allāh (Allāh bless him and give him peace) said:

> He who loves to meet Allāh, Allāh loves to meet him. And he who detests the meeting with Allāh, Allāh detests meeting him (*Bukhārī, Muslim*).

The Nature of Love of Allāh

The inclining of the heart toward something that gives it pleasure is called love (*maḥabba*). *Maḥabba* consists of two kinds: physical love (*maḥabba ṭabʿī*) and intellectual love (*maḥabba ʿaqlī*). Physical love is not a voluntary or volitional condition. Its occurrence and continued existence are non-volitional. Often non-volitional acts are not lasting and are merely transitory. It is for this reason that physical love is not commanded. The origination and continued existence of intellectual love, on the other hand, are volitional. It is therefore a state that can endure. Intellectual love is therefore commanded. It is this kind of love that is superior and preferable. Since the source of physical love is emotion, it is a passing state.

The Causes of Love of Allāh

There are three factors giving rise to the love of something: *iḥsān* (kindness and support)—kindness shown gives rise to love of the one showing kindness; *jamāl* (beauty)—beauty in something brings about attraction that gives rise to love of it; and *kamāl* (perfection)—perfection in a thing also induces love of it. These three attributes par excellence exist only in Allāh Most High. The love of Allāh endures as long as these attributes endure. Insofar as the object of true love (Allāh Most High) is concerned, these attributes are eternal. They will endure forever; hence, love for Him is perpetual. Since the existence of attributes in the state of perfection is not found independently (*bi 'l-dhāt*) in any being other than Allāh Most High, the perfected saints (*kāmilūn*) cannot have intellectual love for anyone other than Allāh Most High. Physical love is possible toward others, but the love toward Allāh Most High that has been commanded is intellectual love. The terminology of the Qur'ān and ḥadīth describes this form of love as *ḥubb.*

This should not be understood to mean that the perfected saints are without physical love. However, in them intellectual love is dominant. At times physical love in the perfected saints exceeds the love in those in whom physical love is dominant, but intellectual love remains dominant in spite of this comparatively higher degree of physical love. At times, physical love becomes dominant in even the perfected saints, but this is very rare.

In short, the perfected saints are perfect in both intellectual and physical love—the former being dominant, while in others physical love is dominant. Although this attribute of excellence [in the perfected saints] is not a goal in itself, it nevertheless is praiseworthy. Those devoid of both these aspects of love are in danger. Love of Allāh is thus essential. Obedience without love of Allāh is not sufficient as there is no resolution and firmness in such acts of obedience devoid of love.

Acquiring Love of Allāh

Constant remembrance and contemplation of the attributes and bounties of Allāh Most High will induce the desired love for Him. Compliance with the laws of the Sharīʿa and much remembrance of Allāh expel the love of others from the heart, making way for the exclusive Love of Allāh Most High.

Longing

Allāh Most High says:

> Those who long to meet with Allāh (should take solace in the knowledge that), indeed, the Time of Allāh is approaching (Qur'ān 29:5).

The Messenger of Allāh (Allāh bless him and give him peace) said:

> I ask of You [O Allāh!] for the sight of Your Face and the longing to meet with You (*Nasā'ī*).

The Nature of Longing

The condition of natural desire (eagerness), which is a physical state, to behold and fully comprehend a beloved object whose perfection is only partially known is termed longing (*shawq*).

Longing is the initial stage of love of Allāh; at a later stage it develops into affection (*uns*). At this later stage the conditions prevailing during the state of longing do not remain. Among such conditions are profuse weeping and absorption in thought to such a degree that this condition asserts its dominance. Some [along the journey] consider such conditions to be the goal [of the journey], and hence become depressed when these are reduced in the state of affection. However, there is no need to be concerned with this reduction in such feelings because the goal is not that the state of longing be perpetual—that one should at all times be engulfed in this state. The purpose is not to eliminate natural desires, nor is the purpose to create a constant throb in the heart. The Messenger of Allāh (Allāh bless him and give him peace) explained the limit of longing in the following way: "[O Allāh!] I petition You for [the state of] longing to meet You, such longing that is devoid of hardship and that does not harm, such longing that is not a trial leading astray" (*Nasā'ī*).

Sometimes excessive affection and love bring about destruction. It brings about a disturbance in righteous acts, which are in fact the medium for attaining Divine Proximity. The true goal is achieved via the agency of carrying out the Divine Commands. Excessive longing and *ʿishq* (overwhelming love) interfere with the means. At times when longing is overpowering, one transgresses the limits of reverence and makes such statements that are irreverent. Most lovers (*ʿushshāq*) are guilty of irreverent statements they utter in states of ecstasy (*ḥāl*). This irreverence is harmful, although such disrespect uttered in ecstasy is forgiven. But, it is not a condition of perfection (*kamāl*).

The Messenger of Allāh (Allāh bless him and give him peace) was perfect in obedience, reverence, and love; hence he made the supplication mentioned above.

Acquiring Longing

Longing, a necessary corollary of love of Allāh, is acquired by inculcating love of Allāh Most High.

The Nature of Affection

Affection (*uns*) is a state of delight and pleasure induced by true recognition of certain known attributes of an object. In this state the object is known only partially, part of it being hidden. The known attributes on which the gaze is focused induce the condition of affection.

Affection is also a necessary corollary of love of Allāh. Its acquisition is along with love of Allāh Most High.

Fear

Allāh Most High commands in the Noble Qur'ān:

> And fear Me! (Qur'ān 16:2)

The Messenger of Allāh (Allāh bless him and give him peace) said:

> He who fears sets off (on the journey) at night. He who sets off at night reaches the destination. Lo! The merchandise of Allāh is costly. Lo! The merchandise of Allāh is Paradise (*Tirmidhī*).

The Nature of Fear

Fear (*khawf*) is the painful condition of the heart that arises as a result of thinking of something reprehensible and the fear of it materializing. The nature of fear consists of the possibility of punishment (*ʿitāb*). This possibility extends to every person, for he may be overtaken by punishment. This is the extent of fear that has been commanded and imposed upon the servant. This extent, fearing the possibility of punishment, is a compulsory condition of faith. It is also known as intellectual fear (*khawf ʿaqlī*). At the behest of sin, this faculty has to be put into operation. The warnings and punishments of Allāh Most High should be recalled and considered so as to save oneself from sin. This degree of fear is obligatory (*farḍ*). Its non-existence induces and involves one in sin. It is the medium of exhorting toward virtue and steering one away from sin.

Allāh Most High has combined the noble attributes of guidance (*hidāya*), mercy (*raḥma*), knowledge (*ʿilm*) and contentment (*riḍā*) for those who are imbued with His fear. All beings fear the one who fears Allāh Most High. Allāh Most High has stated that in the servant, two fears will not combine. This means that the servant of Allāh who on earth entertains fear of Allāh Most High will be fearless in the Hereafter, and he who had no fear of Allāh Most High on earth will be overtaken by fear and calamity. In this regard, the Messenger of Allāh (Allāh bless him and give him peace) said, "On the Day of Resurrection, every eye will be crying except the eye that refrained from gazing at what Allāh Most High had prohibited, and the eye that stood guard in the Path of Allāh, and the eye from which emerged a teardrop equal in size to the head of a gnat out of fear of Allāh Most High."

In a ḥadīth of *Mishkāt al-Maṣabīḥ*, it is said that Allāh will make the fire of Hell unlawful for such a person. In the ḥadīth it is also stated that on the Day of Resurrection, Allāh Most High will command the angels to remove from the Fire anyone who had at any time or occasion feared Allāh (*Tirmidhī*).

Fear is thus obligatory upon every believer. There are two reasons for this: the possibility of one committing voluntarily an act of disobedience in the future and the possibility of some act of disobedience having been voluntarily committed, which could have been caught had one paid attention, but due to negligence, one's attention has been diverted. Such diversion is also a voluntary act of disobedience.

It is a fact that the robber, because of the fear of being apprehended, abstains from robbery; the child, because of the fear of punishment, abstains from mischief; and people, because of the fear of being fined, refrain from violation of law. When fear is effaced, anarchy is the consequence in the land. Fear severs the roots of all evil, while at the same time it is the medium of all obedience.

The manner in which to acquire the fear of Allāh Most High is to consider His wrath and punishment.

Hope

Allāh Most High says:

> Do not despair of the mercy of Allāh (Qur'ān 39:53).

The Messenger of Allāh (Allāh bless him and give him peace) said:

> If even the unbeliever should realize the extent of Allāh's mercy, he [too] would not lose hope of Paradise (*Bukhārī, Muslim*).

The Nature of Hope

Hope (*rajā'*) is the state of the heart's tranquility that develops as a result of one's yearning for the desirable objects of Divine Grace (*faḍl*), forgiveness (*maghfira*), bounty (*ni'ma*), and Paradise, while devising ways and means for their attainment. Thus, one who remains in expectation of mercy and Paradise, but does not adopt the means of their acquisition (righteous deeds, repentance, and so forth), will not attain the goal of hope. He remains, on the contrary, in deception. He is like the one who, in spite of not sowing the seeds, expects to reap the crop. He dwells in empty desire. The manner of acquiring hope is to reflect about the vastness of Allāh's mercy and His munificence.

Abstinence

Allāh Most High says:

> So that you do not grieve over what you have lost nor become proud over what you have (Qur'ān 57:23).

The Messenger of Allāh (Allāh bless him and give him peace) said:

> The first virtue of this nation is firm faith (*yaqīn*) and abstinence (*zuhd*), and the first corruption of this nation is miserliness (*bukhl*) and vain hopes (*amal*) (Bayhaqī, *Shuʿab al-īmān*).

The Nature of Abstinence

Abstinence (*zuhd*) is to refrain from an object of desire in the pursuit of a nobler objective—refraining from the desire of the world and pursuing the desire of the Hereafter.

The basis of abstinence is the light and knowledge that Allāh Most High inspires in the heart of man. As a result, his breast expands and he realizes with clarity that the world with all that is in it is more contemptible than the wing of a fly and that only the Hereafter is noble and everlasting. When this light is acquired, the worthlessness of the world fully dawns upon man. The effect of abstinence is the attainment of contentment upon the acquisition of the bare necessities of life. Thus the abstinent (*zāhid*) is satisfied with the bare necessities in the same way as the traveler is satisfied with the necessities that he takes along on his journey.

Abstinence is not abstention from pleasures. Reduction of pleasures is a sufficient condition of abstinence. In other words, one should not be engrossed in pleasures. Constantly hankering after luxuries is contrary to abstinence. On the other hand, acquisition of luxuries, without undue effort and arrangement, is of the bounties of Allāh Most High, for which thanksgiving must be offered. Along with granting comfort to the self, effort too should be imposed on it.

In truth, gold and silver and the world with all its possessions, in the sight of one whose gaze is focused on Allāh, are of no value. The Messenger of Allāh (Allāh bless him and give him peace) never preferred the world for himself nor for those close to him. Whatever creation possesses is the material of the world. It is essential to sever one's hope from all things. He who is successful in this objective will attain tranquility because both heart and body find rest and peace in abstinence.

The manner in which to acquire abstinence is to meditate on the defects, harms, and ephemeral nature of the world, as well as to reflect on the benefits and the everlasting nature of the Hereafter.

Trust in Allāh

Allāh Most High says:

> In Allāh should the believers have trust (Qur'ān 3:160).

The Messenger of Allāh (Allāh bless him and give him peace) said:

> When you ask, ask of Allāh. And when you seek help, seek help from Allāh (*Tirmidhī, Aḥmad*).

The Nature of Trust in Allāh

The heart's inherent trust in the Creator alone is called *tawakkul*. The meaning of *tawakkul* is expressed by the term *tawkīl* (to appoint a *wakīl*, or trustee). When one lacks the understanding and ability for something, then another is appointed to undertake the task. Such appointment of an agent to act on one's behalf is the meaning of *tawkīl*. Trust then is to act in accordance with Allāh's plan: to adopt the principles and commands of the Sharīʿa, and to resign oneself to Him. In every act or task, the means required for the task must be employed within the confines of the Sharīʿa, and one's trust must be placed in Allāh Most High.

The Three Fundamentals of Trust

Gnosis

Gnosis, or *maʿrifa*, consists of affirming the oneness of Allāh Most High, which entails affirming the fact that besides Allāh there is nothing worthy of worship, that He is Incomparable, that He has no partner, that all sovereignty belongs to Him, that all praise and glorification belongs to Him, and that He has power over all things. This conception of oneness acknowledges that Allāh Most High possesses such perfect power and wisdom that makes Him worthy of all praise and glory. Sincere and honest belief in this conception of oneness establishes true faith in the heart. The effect of faith establishing itself in the heart is trust (*tawakkul*). The condition essential for achieving this trust is sincere acknowledgment of oneness. The meaning of sincere acknowledgment is that this oneness permeates the heart to such a degree that there remains no room in one's heart to entertain any other concept.

Reliance

The *ḥāla,* or state of reliance (*tawakkul*), is to resign oneself to Allāh Most High. Assign all affairs to Him and maintain the heart in the state of peace and tranquility. It entails turning away from all and everything other than Allāh. Upon Allāh Most High being made the trustee, one resigns in full confidence. Allāh Most High, the Trustee, is full of wisdom and is the Benefactor and Protector of the one who has placed trust in Him. There is therefore no need for the heart to toss about in doubt and uncertainty. He will not allow your enemy to vanquish you. In this way when one fully realizes that sustenance, death, life and all affairs of creation are within the direct power and control of Allāh Most High, there is absolutely no cause for the heart to labor in uncertainty and suffer any lack of confidence.

Toil

The ignorant toil under the misconception that trust entails abstention from effort, the means, and material agencies. This idea of trust is highly erroneous. Trust does not advocate shunning or abstaining from the material agencies that Allāh Most High has created and made subservient to man. Shunning the legitimate use of the material means and agencies for legitimate purposes and needs is not lawful according to the Sharīʿa.

Acquiring Trust

The way in which to acquire trust is by contemplating the bounties of Allāh Most High, His Promises, and past occasions in which Allāh granted one success.

Restraint

Restraint (*qanāʿa*) means abstention from desires. Contemplating the transitory and perishable nature of the world inculcates restraint and contentment.

Forbearance

Forbearance (*ḥilm*) means to hold in check the self in the face of distasteful events. This quality of forbearance is acquired by the eradication of anger. One has to contemplate constantly the remedies for anger. This has been explained above in the chapter on the Blameworthy Character Traits.

Patience

Allāh Most High says:

> O people of faith, adopt patience (Qur'ān 3:200).

The Messenger of Allāh (Allāh bless him and give him peace) said:

> A believer is to be marveled at because every condition of his is good. This is exclusive to the believer. If he attains happiness, he is thankful, and that is good for him, and if calamity overtakes him, he is patient, and that is good for him (*Muslim*).

The Nature of Patience

In man are two conflicting forces. The one force impels him toward religion and righteousness, while the other drives him toward base desires. Asserting the religious force and subduing the force of base desires is called patience (*ṣabr*). In the state of patience, the religious force in man asserts its dominance over the force of base desires. Its definition is as follows: maintaining control over the lower self in the face of such things that the lower self abhors.

There are three kinds of patience: patience in the practice of righteous deeds (*ṣabr ʿala ʾl-ʿamal*), patience while engaging in righteous deeds (*ṣabr fī ʾl-ʿamal*), and patience in refraining from indulging in the unlawful (*ṣabr ʿani ʾl-ʿamal*).

The first type entails being firm and constant in practicing righteous deeds.

The second type entails having patience while engaging in a righteous deed: the lower self is held in check and prevented from distraction while engaged in an act of virtue. Acts of worship have to be discharged adequately by the observance of the principles and rules pertaining to them. Full attention has to be directed toward the act.

The third type entails having patience in the non-commission of any [unlawful] act or to restrain the lower self from indulging in the prohibitions of Allāh Most High.

Blessing and Hardships

Blessings (*niʿma*) produce delight and happiness, which in turn result in love of Allāh, the Benefactor. On the other hand, hardships (*muṣība*) produce frustration and grief. Thus, the occasion of patience is in the face of hardship. Hardship is the condition detested by the lower self. This condition is of two kinds: the form of hardship and true hardship.

Grief and frustration follow in the wake of true hardship, which is the consequence of sin. Hardship that brings about the strengthening of one's bond with Allāh and elevates one's spiritual condition is not true hardship. It is merely a semblance of hardship. It increases one's submission to Allāh Most High. The gnostics do perceive hardship. In fact their sense of perception is sharper, but due to their gaze being on Allāh Most High their grief and sorrow do not exceed the limits.

Difficulties are a means for the expiation of many sins. At times Allāh Most High wishes to bestow a special rank of elevation to a servant, but the servant lacks the ability to attain that lofty rank solely by virtue of his righteous deeds. Allāh Most High then afflicts him with some hardship by virtue of which he attains the desired lofty rank. It appears in a noble ḥadīth that on the Day of Resurrection, the people of good fortune and happiness (*niʿma*) will be jealous of those who underwent hardship and sorrow (*muṣība*). They will envy them and wish, "Would that our skins were cut to bits with scissors so that today we could have attained the ranks bestowed to the people of hardship."

It is also narrated in a noble ḥadīth that he who exacts his vengeance, Allāh Most High assigns his affair to himself. As for the one who adopts patience, Allāh Most High exacts vengeance on his behalf. Allāh then might award him in this world or might, on the Day of Resurrection, waive his punishment entirely. Allāh Most High states in the Noble Qur'ān, "When a hardship afflicts them, they say: *Innā li 'Llāhi wa innā ilayhi rājiʿūn* (Verily, we are for Allāh and unto Him will we return)" (Qur'ān 2:156).

The purport of this verse is that one should engage in the *dhikr* of *Innā li 'Llāhi wa innā ilayhi rājiʿūn* at the time of difficulty and hardship. One should meditate upon the meaning of this statement—that we are the exclusive property of Allāh, we belong to Him, and He has the full right to utilize and dispose of His property as He sees fit. We are, therefore, content with the decree of Allāh.

When hardship afflicts one, he should first remember his sins. Such remembrance of shortcomings and faults will fortify one against depression during the hardship. One will then realize the correctness of the affliction and accept it without complaint. One will regret and not protest. Secondly, meditate upon the reward that Allāh has promised for hardship. Remembering this reward will lessen the grief and keep one resolute in the state of hardship. Never complain or entertain the impression that Allāh Most High has become displeased with you. This impression is dangerous because it weakens the bond with Allāh Most High, and by degrees one's relationship with Allāh Most High becomes obliterated.

Consider hardship as either a punishment or a trial and contemplate its reward. At the time of hardship, the Sharīʿa calls to patience and steadfastness. For every hardship, the compensation will be good. There is, most certainly, benefit in hardship, in this world as well as in the Hereafter, although one may not be able to understand the worldly benefit therein.

Acquiring Patience

Patience is inculcated by weakening the desires of lust and emotion.

Gratitude

Allāh Most High says:

> Be grateful unto Me (Qur'ān 2:152).

The Messenger of Allāh (Allāh bless him and give him peace) said:

> If happiness reaches him [the believer], he is grateful (*Muslim*).

The Nature of Gratitude

Accepting that all benefit is from the True Benefactor (*al-Munᶜim al-Ḥaqīqī*), the effect of which is to be happy with the Benefactor and be ever ready to render obedience to Him, is the meaning of gratitude (*shukr*). This entails acceptance of the fact that all benefit is from Allāh, the True Benefactor. This acceptance induces happiness with the Benefactor, and eagerness to carry out the commands of the Benefactor and to abstain from His prohibitions. One should consider all benefit, goodness, and pleasant conditions as the bounties of Allāh and regard these to be in greater measure than what one really deserves. Praise is to be offered to Allāh and His bounties should not be employed in evil and sin. His favors should be used in obtaining His good pleasure. This is the true meaning of gratitude.

This conception of gratitude will be understood only when one has realized the purpose underlying creation and the functions of the various aspects of creation. For instance, the eye is a blessing from Allāh Most High. Gratitude in relation to it is to employ it correctly—to employ it only in lawful ways, such as reading the Glorious Qur'ān, acquiring knowledge, studying the wonderful creation of Allāh so as to learn and realize the greatness and splendor of Allāh Most High, and so forth. The gratitude of the eye further demands that it be restrained from glancing at and viewing objects that Allāh Most High has prohibited.

Likewise, the ear is a blessing. Gratitude in relation to it is to employ it correctly, such as in listening to the remembrance (*dhikr*) of Allāh, to such talks that remind one of the Hereafter, and to prevent it from listening to evil, nonsensical, and useless talk.

The tongue is a blessing. Gratitude in relation to it is to employ it in remembrance, in expressing glorification, praise, and thanks to Allāh, and to restrain it from complaining in adversity and from all evil in general. It is highly inappropriate and sinful for such a worthless slave as man to complain about any condition that Allāh Most High, the True King, has imposed on him. A word of gratitude emanating from the tongue is recorded as an act of obedience.

Mere expression of gratitude with the tongue unaccompanied by the true state of gratitude of the heart is only lip service. It is essential that along with verbal expression of gratitude, the heart should value and honor the blessing of the Benefactor. Mere verbal gratitude will be as the outer casing, as the outer skin that is its external form. The essence of gratitude is that the honor and appreciation of the Benefactor and the blessing are ingrained in the heart.

The initial stage of gratitude is at the intellectual level. In other words, it is the correct understanding of the true meaning of gratitude and the realization of the honor of the Benefactor. The final stage of gratitude is the manifestation of its effect on one's body, movements, and all states. In short, the beliefs, acts of worship, mundane acts, and moral and social life of the one who is truly grateful to Allāh will be in conformity with the Sharīʿa.

Acquiring Gratitude

Gratitude is acquired by contemplating the bounties of Allāh Most High. Every blessing is to be related to Him. By degrees such meditation will inspire love of Allāh in the heart, the result of which will be the attainment of the perfect stage of gratitude.

Truthfulness

Allāh Most High says:

> Verily, the believers are those who believe in Allāh and His Messenger. Thereafter they have no doubt and they strive in the Path of Allāh with their wealth and their lives. Verily, they are the *ṣādiqūn* (truthful ones) (Qur'ān 49:15).

The following is told in a noble ḥadīth:

> The Prophet (Allāh bless him and give him peace) passed by Abū Bakr (Allāh

be well pleased with him) as he was cursing some of his slaves. The Messenger of Allāh (Allāh bless him and give him peace) turned toward him and said, "People who curse and people who are truthful?" Abū Bakr (Allāh be well pleased with him) said, "I will not repeat it" (Bayhaqī, *Shuʿab al-īmān*).

The Nature of Truthfulness

The nature of truthfulness (*ṣidq*) consists of developing an acquired rank until it is perfected. The meaning of truthfulness is steadfastness. It is for this reason that a perfected saint (*walī kāmil*) is called a truthful one. In all states, acts, and speech the perfected saint is well grounded. He has realized the state of perfection. In the Sharīʿa, the conception of truthfulness includes actions, speech, and states and conditions. Truthfulness in regard to speech is that talk should be firm and true according to reality. One imbued with this quality is called "truthful in speech." Truthfulness in regard to actions is that every act be in conformity with the command of the Sharīʿa and not in conflict with it. One whose acts are at all times in conformity with the Sharīʿa is termed "truthful in acts." Truthfulness in regard to one's state or condition is that all conditions should be in accordance with the Sunna. Conditions that are in conflict with the Sunna are false. One whose states are in accordance with the Sunna is called "truthful in states."

The states of truthfulness are such that their effect is enduring. The influence of the states of truthfulness is lasting and dominant. They are not of a temporary nature. They should not exist in a person one day and be absent another. Nor does this mean that such states should overwhelm one perpetually. Rather, the effect or influence of these states of truthfulness should abide, become a station, and not fade.

The summary of what has been explained is that one should develop the acts of worship or obedience to the stage of perfection. For example, perform prayer in such a way that it could be described in the Sharīʿa as a perfect prayer—a prayer performed in observance of all the external and internal rules and etiquette. The same should apply to all other acts of obedience and worship. The implementation of this way is truthfulness.

Acquiring Truthfulness

Truthfulness is dependent upon knowledge of the factors that produce perfection. Therefore, one has to be alert at all times and compensate for one's shortcomings. An effort is to be made to rectify poorly performed obligations. Constancy in improving and perfecting one's acts will ensure within a short while the perfect state of truthfulness.

Consigning One's Affairs

Allāh Most High says:

> I consign my affair to Allāh. Verily He sees all (His) servants (Qur'ān 40:44).

The Messenger of Allāh (Allāh bless him and give him peace) said:

> When you arise in the morning do not fret about the evening, and when it is evening do not fret about the morning (*Bukhārī*).

The Nature of Consigning One's Affairs

Tafwīḍ is to consign one's affairs to Allāh Most High. He may do with one as He desires. One's gaze and hope should be on none besides Allāh. While employing the means and the agencies, the result of all things should be left to Allāh Most High.

To consign one's affairs does not mean shunning the means and the agencies that Allāh Most High has created for the acquisition and handling of affairs. It merely means that one's confidence and hope should be on none besides Allāh Most High. The result of the employment of the means and agencies should be left to Allāh Most High. In affairs not related to means and agencies, consignment should be adopted from the very beginning. In such matters, one should not adopt planning and scheming.

To plan and scheme is the cause of all worry, because of it being expected a project should proceed according to the set plan and program arranged for it. If the result is contrary to expectation, worry and frustration are the consequence. The schemes initiated by man mostly consist of matters beyond the control of his will. It is therefore childish to scheme about things not within one's will. It is for this reason that the Friends of Allāh shun scheming. They resign themselves entirely and submit to the pleasure of Allāh Most High.

It is necessary to abandon one's own scheme of operation and resign oneself to Allāh. This even applies to the development of one's spiritual condition. When treading the spiritual path of development one should not initiate one's own scheme. Assign everything to Him. Bestowal or the elimination of spiritual states and conditions should be assigned to Him. The seeker of Allāh should give up his planning for the plan of Allāh Most High. In other words, he has to adopt total and perfect submission and surrender—becoming a perfect slave of Allāh Most High.

Acquiring Consignment of One's Affairs

When confronted with an event that is not to one's liking, immediately think that it is an act of Allāh and most assuredly that there is wisdom and good in it. In the beginning it will be difficult to acquire this attitude. However, constant reflection produces the eradication of effort, and this approach then becomes a natural condition in the Friends of Allāh.

Contentment

Allāh Most High says:

> Allah is pleased with them and they are pleased with Him (Qur'ān 98:8).

The Messenger of Allāh (Allāh bless him and give him peace) said:

> Of the good fortune of man is his contentment with what Allāh has decreed for him (*Tirmidhī, Aḥmad*).

The Nature of Contentment

This consists of total submission and contentment with the Decree. One should neither by word or deed object to fate. Contentment (*riḍa*) develops to such a lofty degree that its domination permeates one's being. In this high state of contentment, hardship recedes and is not considered as such. The state of contentment in which even pain is not felt is called "natural contentment." The state in which contentment prevails along with the sensation of pain is called "intellectual contentment."

The first state is a physical condition whose acquisition is not obligatory.

The second state is an intellectual condition whose acquisition is obligatory.

Contentment with fate is commanded and exhorted so as to inculcate in one the qualities of perseverance and satisfaction when afflicted by adversity and hardship. When contentment has been inculcated, adversity will be taken in stride with pleasure and without feeling any undue hardship. This is so because the intelligence alerts one to the superior results of such contentment in the face of adversity. The result of such contentment is future reward.

This will be better understood by means of an illustration. A physician prescribes a bitter remedy to a patient or may even insist on an operation. The patient, bearing in mind his future recovery and health, willingly submits to the treatment. He is not only pleased with the physician but feels indebted to him.

Similarly he who firmly believes that Allāh Most High will grant a reward for every difficulty and sorrow experienced here will most certainly be filled with pleasure and happiness. The reward for contentment is of such a nature that all difficulty fades into nothingness. It is improper to desire anything contrary to what Allāh Most High has willed and decreed for the servant. When Allāh Most High considers adversity and difficulty appropriate and advantageous for us, then we as His servants have no valid reason for displeasure and grief.

Whatever state Allāh Most High chooses for a servant, that is best for him. Seeing another in a more prosperous condition than himself, man yearns for such prosperity and is not contented with his own lot. But reflection will prove to one that the condition chosen for one by Allāh Most High is best.

It should be observed that supplication is not contrary to contentment. The people of Allāh resort to supplication because of the Divine Command. In this way they profess their state of total submission and surrender to Allāh. They therefore do not insist on the attainment of what is being supplicated for. In all states and circumstances, they are fully pleased with the choice of Allāh Most High, whether their supplication is accepted or not. Non-acceptance never causes dissatisfaction in them. This is the sign of true contentment.

Acquiring Contentment

Contentment is an effect of the love of Allāh. Consequently there is no other means of acquiring this quality [except by means of love], as contentment is a necessary corollary of love.

Annihilation

Annihilation (*fanā'*) consists of the elimination of evil deeds and lowly attributes of the flesh. In other words, annihilation is refraining from sin and the expulsion from the heart of all love other than Divine Love—expulsion of greed, lust, desire, vanity, show, and so forth. In the state of annihilation, the reality of the true and only relationship asserts itself in the mind. One realizes and feels that the only real relationship is with Allāh Most High.

Acquiring Annihilation

This lofty state of annihilation is attainable through spiritual struggle and remembrance in abundance—remembrance by means of both the tongue and heart.

Annihilation of Annihilation

At times, the seeker becomes oblivious of his state of annihilation. This unawareness is termed annihilation of annihilation (*fanā' al-fanā'*). According to some this term is used for perpetuity (*baqā'*). In this state the realization of one's condition of selflessness disappears.

Making righteous deeds one's natural disposition and perfecting the praiseworthy character traits is also termed *baqā'*.

The state of annihilation of annihilation is realized by abundant remembrance (*dhikr*) and constant contemplation (*fikr*).

IV

Guidance & Admonition

Obedience to the Messenger of Allāh
(Allāh bless him and give him peace)
is imperative. Such obedience is essential
in word, act, and intention because love of
Allāh Most High is not possible without
obedience to the Messenger Muḥammad.

—Khwājā Naṣīr al-Dīn Chirāgh Dehlawī

Attaining Proximity to Allāh

There are three paths by which one can attain proximity to Allāh Most High. These are explained in detail as follows.

The Longest Path (Aṭwal)

This consists of abundant fasts, prayer, recitation, pilgrimages, *jihād,* and so forth. This is the path of [a class of Friends of Allāh known as] the *akhyār* (good) and *ṣulaḥā'* (pious).

The Middle Path (awsaṭ)

In addition to the above acts of worship are engagements in spiritual struggle and exercises, elimination of blameworthy character traits, and the acquisition of praiseworthy character traits. The majority of men traveling along the path of *suluk* become *wāṣil* (attain the goal of Divine Proximity) via this second path. This is the path of the *abrār* (righteous).

The Least and Shortest Path (Aqall wa Aqrab)

This is the path of love (*ʿishq*). Spiritual exercises and mingling with people are suffocating to the spiritual traveler on this path. Remembrance, contemplation, gratitude, and longing are the intellectual occupations of the traveler wandering along the Path of Love. The traveler on this path becomes *wāṣil* by this method. Purification of the lower self and adornment of the heart and soul are realized by the method of love. They have no interest in spiritual unveilings (*kashf*) and miracles (*karāmāt*). They are totally immersed in: "Die before your death." This third way is the way of the Shaṭāriyya.

[Shaṭāriyya is a class of the Friends of Allāh (*awliyā'*) who are naturally endowed with strong emotion. Their purified emotion is permeated with Divine Love, which is loftier than the intellectual love that other Muslims have in varying degrees for Allāh Most High. The Divine Love in these Friends of Allāh is so overwhelming that the most difficult exercise is no struggle for them. They are spurred on by pure Divine Love, which makes them totally oblivious of everything else. This does not mean that they are oblivious of the Laws of the Sharīʿa and the Sunna. On the contrary, they are extremely scrupulous in the Sharīʿa and the Sunna because they are both related to the Beloved Essence. They renounce the world physically and derive the greatest emotional and intellectual pleasure in solitude far from people. In fact, they flee from people as a deer flees when it sees humans. As a result of their extreme yearning for Allāh Most High—which is in an emotional state—they reach Him very quickly, and sometimes, Allāh Most High keeps them "at bay" by engulfing them in many difficulties, hardships, grief, and sorrow. But they persevere, never flinching for even a moment. Instead, they derive solace from all the hardships in their spiritual journey. In short, they are immersed in the love of Allah Most High. (translator)]

Dying Before Death

At the time of death, the dying man possesses certain attributes whose inculcation is understood from the following aphorism: "Die before your death." The attributes that are in the perfect state in the dying man are *tawba* (repentance), *zuhd* (abstention), *qanāʿa* (contentment), *tawakkul* (trust in Allāh), *ʿazla* (solitude), *tawajjuh ila 'Llāh* (attention directed to Allāh), *ṣabr* (patience), *riḍā* (being pleased with Allāh), *dhikr* (remembrance of Allāh), and *murāqaba* (meditation).

Among the Shaṭāriyya the significant feature is meditation. One has to inculcate the above qualities, which overtake a dying person to a high degree. Repentance—to emerge from all evil, as is the position at the time of death; abstention—to shun the world and everything in it, as is the case at death; reliance—to shun all normal worldly agencies, as is the case at death; solitude—to sever all ties with creation, as is the case at death; abstention from lowly desires—to be satisfied, as is the case at death; to rivet one's attention toward only Allāh Most High, as is the case at death; patience—to shun pleasures, as is the case at death; contentment—to abstain from pleasing the lower self, and to be pleased with Allāh, and to submit entirely to Allāh Most High, as is the case at death. This is the conception of "Die before your death."

One has to transform one's condition so as to be saturated with the conception of "death before death." In this earthly life, the body is on earth, but the spirit should be directed to the Hereafter and be in communion with Allāh Most High. Possession of even the kingdom of the earth should not affect one's heart. The heart should be empty of the world at all times. The sign that this lofty state has settled over one is total abstention from everything branded as evil by the Sharīʿa. The mind, tongue, and the whole body have to be sealed from evil. The heart is to be emptied of all things other than Allāh Most High. It has to be adorned with praiseworthy character traits.

A man dwelling in this lofty state of purity and communion with Allāh Most High is always aloof from gatherings of futility. Whatever diverts the mind of the seeker of Allāh from the remembrance of Allāh is vain and nonsensical. The seeker refrains from association with men of falsehood and corruption (*bāṭil*). One who does not pursue the Path in quest of Allāh is in fact a man of corruption.

O beloved one! This then is the meaning of "Die before your death." This is the way of the Messenger of Allāh (Allāh bless him and give him peace). This is the life that the Messenger of Allāh (Allāh bless him and give him peace) desired for his nation.

Dominance of Praiseworthy Character Traits

The sign that praiseworthy character traits have gained dominance and that one has gained proficiency in these lofty attributes is the ability to employ correctly and naturally these attributes with the utmost ease. Once one has reached this stage, it is evidence that the lofty attributes have become firmly grounded in one.

Passing Thoughts

Thoughts that cross the heart of man are called *khawāṭir* (sg. *khāṭir*). Such thoughts are at times virtuous and at times evil. These thoughts emanate from different sources. Virtue is inspired into the heart sometimes by Allāh Most High, sometimes by an angel named Mulhim [the Inspirer], and sometimes even virtue is whispered into the heart by the devil. Evil assaulting the heart sometimes emanates from the devil, sometimes from the lower self, and at times from Allāh Most High.

Pious inspirations from Allāh Most High serve the purpose of honoring one or for establishing some proof. The evil thought that comes from Allāh Most High appears as a test and to impose some labor and effort on one. From the angel Mulhim ever emanates goodness alone, since this is his function—to guide toward virtue.

Virtue or the good thought emerging from the devil is deception. He casts his spell in the form of a good thought, but in reality it is evil designed to divert one from a greater virtue by involving one in a lesser virtue. The purpose of evil emanating from the devil is to deceive and disgrace man.

Evil emanating from the lower self is meant to mislead man and to divert him from the truth. The good that issues from the lower self is extremely negligible. It is comparable to that of the devil.

Distinguishing the Signs of Evil from Allāh, the Devil, and the Lower Self

If the evil thought is from Allāh Most High, it is recognized by its firmness and one's total inability to combat it. One will discover that one is unable to ward it off. If the evil that afflicts the heart is firm and retains constancy, being of a solid unchanging form that makes the lower self extremely restless in the desire to commit the evil while at the same time all effort and means of combating the evil are made useless in the face of the onslaught of the evil, then such an evil thought is from Allāh Most High. The remedy for such a thought is nothing but to petition Allāh Most High, seeking His aid and protection, humbling oneself and shedding tears of concern and regret. This is a trial from Allāh Most High. Only His aid will be of any good.

If the thought of evil is not as pressing and severe, as is described above, but remains static, then it is from the lower self.

If a thought of evil assaults the heart after having sinned and it occurs vehemently, then such evil is from Allāh Most High and its purpose is to disgrace the sinner and act as a punishment for having sinned. If, after having sinned, the thought of evil occurs to one, but not vehemently—it enters feebly—then such evil is from the devil, provided that it disappears or is weakened by engagement in remembrance. With regard to this, the Messenger of Allāh (Allāh bless him and give him peace) said, "Verily, the devil clings onto the heart of man. When man remembers Allāh, the devil retreats (from the heart). When man becomes neglectful of Allāh's remembrance, the devil asserts himself with his whisperings (into the heart of man)" (Bukhārī without chain [*taʿlīqan*], Bayhaqī, *Shuʿab al-īmān*).

If the evil thought that assaulted the heart after having sinned does not disappear or weaken by remembrance, then such a thought is directed by the lower self. The devil was the victim of such misguidance by the lower self. When he proclaimed his greatness on the occasion of his refusal to prostrate to Ādam (peace be upon him) as commanded. Neither could his remembrance ward off the evil thought of his lower self, nor did the exhortation of Allāh Most High benefit him. The cause of this rebellion of the devil's lower self was the absence of slavehood [*ʿabdiyya*: the state of total submission—being a slave—to another]. The devil further lacked humility; hence nothing was of benefit to him. He possessed no true insight; hence, his obedience and his worship were mere bodily exercises shorn of the true insight that is in the heart of faith. This condition of the devil became manifest with his rebellion. If he had possessed the insight of faith, he would not have engaged in disputation, but would have submitted and derived pleasure from such submission and true obedience. Argumentation, disputation, and doubt always occur prior to *mushāhada* [true, certain, and established knowledge].

If a virtuous thought settles firmly over the heart and one is unable to attain peace of mind without performing the act of virtue, then that good thought is from Allāh. It will also be from Allāh if the virtuous thought occurs after spiritual struggle and worship, or if the virtuous thought happens to be related to the principles and acts of the *bāṭin* [the internal dimension of man that pertains to his spirit]. Allāh says, "And, those who strive in our way, We will most certainly show them our ways" (Qur'ān 29:69).

In other words, Allāh Most High will direct them toward His proximity, reward, and Paradise. This verse is proof of what has been elaborated in regard to the virtue that emanates from Allāh Most High.

If the virtuous thought entering the heart is not as resolute as explained above or it occurs initially without one having resorted to spiritual struggle or the virtue relates to the details of the external acts of worship and righteousness, then such inspiration is from the angel Mulhim.

How to Recognize Whether a Virtuous Thought is from Allāh or the Devil

A virtuous thought having the following ingredients is from the devil: (1) it produces total delight—delight unchecked by fear; (2) it demands haste—the haste it wants is unchecked; (3) it pertains to something whose consequences are not at all considered.

The following five instances are excluded from this rule:

1. Marriage to a virgin
2. Payment of a debt
3. Burial of the dead.
4. Feeding the visitor
5. Repenting for sins

If the virtuous thought is accompanied by delight tempered with fear and one is concerned about the consequences of the act if it is translated into practice, then that virtuous thought is from Allāh Most High. It has also been said that such a virtuous thought is from the angel Mulhim.

Fear in the context of this discussion means concern and anxiety to render the virtue fully and perfectly, observing all the required rules and etiquette pertaining to that act whose thought has occurred. At the same time, one is anxious in regard to the acceptance of the deed—will Allāh Most High accept it or reject it? The meaning of being concerned about the consequences is in relation to guidance, virtue, and hope for reward in the Hereafter. There should be no other motive.

Mulhim is the name of an angel who occupies the right side of the heart, while Waswās is the name of the devil who occupies the left side of the heart of man. A ḥadīth explains this: "When man is born Allāh Most High creates an angel and a devil along with him. The devil makes his abode on the left side of man's heart, and the angel settles on the right side. Both then call upon man" (*Ibn Kathīr*).

Some effort, concern, and remembrance (among which the recitation of *Lā ḥawla wa lā quwwata illa bi 'Llāh* is very efficacious) will suffice to ward off the thought from the devil. Allāh Most High states, "Verily, the scheme of the devil is weak" (Qur'ān 4:76).

The best remedy for the thoughts and whisperings of the devil is to totally ignore them. How does one know that one is ignoring such thoughts of the devil? The recognition of this is that one will not be unduly bothered or vexed when such thoughts assault one. The state of indifference that existed prior to the entry of satanic whispering should also prevail after these thoughts have entered the heart. In fact, the occurrence of satanic whispering is proof of one's faith. Such assaults should therefore be a cause of happiness and not sorrow. When the Noble Companions explained their concern and vexation about these satanic thoughts that afflicted them, the Messenger of Allāh (Allāh bless him and give him peace) said, "This is clear evidence of faith" (*Muslim*). A thief makes an attempt only where there is something of value.

Regarding the desires of the lower self, great effort and great struggle are required. Subjugation of the desires of the lower self is achieved only after struggle. The need to confront the lower self with resolution, wrath, and determination is very important.

There are three ways of combating the desires of the lower self:

1. Preventing it from lust by denying it its nutrition. Its desires should not be fulfilled. Much resistance has to be offered to the lower self. When a wild horse is denied food or its food is reduced, it becomes submissive. It will become subdued, and the lustful demands of the lower self will be ended.
2. The imposition of worship on the lower self also weakens its demands.

An ass becomes weak and submissive if along with denying it food it is given a heavy load. Similarly, the lower self will be transformed from a state of restlessness to tranquility by imposing on it beneficial worship.

3. Seeking the aid of Allāh Most High. Allāh says in the Noble Qur'ān, "Verily, the lower self incites to evil, except when my Lord is merciful (such a lower self will remain obedient)" (Qur'ān 12:53).

Adoption of these three methods with constancy will, Allāh willing, make the lower self obedient and submissive. Man will then be safe from its evil prompting. Even after having gained control of the lower self, one has to be alert at all times. Heedlessness (*ghafla*) is extremely dangerous. It causes the lower self to assert once again its domination and control over man.

The Nature of the Lower Self

In man, there exists the capacity for desire. This capacity is termed the lower self (*nafs*). This capacity includes both virtue and evil. It desires goodness as well as evil. In its development the lower self passes through three stages: the lower self that incites to evil (*nafs ammāra*); the lower self that denounces evil (*nafs lawwāma*); and the lower self that is well pleased (*nafs muṭma'inna*).

Nafs Ammāra

At this stage, the lower self is overpowering in desire for evil, and it feels no regret for its evil acts. This lowly stage is also termed *hawā 'l-nafs.*

Nafs Lawwāma

At this stage, the lower self suffers remorse and regret when afflicted by evil desires.

Nafs Muṭma'inna

At this stage, the lower self is tremendously desirous of virtue.

Types of Thought and Their Rulings

According to a ḥadīth, Allāh Most High overlooks thoughts as long as they are not given practical expression. There are five stages in thought: whim (*hājis*), notion (*khawāṭir*), deliberation (*ḥadīth al-nafs*), inclination (*hamm*), and firm decision (*ʿazm*).

Hājis

A whim (*hājis*) is a thought that in the beginning produces no reaction in the lower self. If one is fortunate to eliminate the thought at this stage, the other four stages will not become relevant.

Khāṭir

If one fails to eliminate the whim and it establishes its presence in the lower self without the latter [i.e., the lower self] plotting to give it practical expression, it [the whim] enters the notion (*khāṭir*) stage.

Ḥadīth al-nafs

At this stage, the lower self considers acting or not acting upon that which has become established in the lower self. It ruminates on the plot without giving preference to any course of action. The thought is now known as deliberation (*ḥadīth al-nafs*).

The ruling (*ḥukm*) on these three stages is no punishment if the thought is evil and no reward if the thought is good. Punishment and reward do not apply to the stages of whim, notion, and deliberation.

Hamm

When the lower self, after having reflected about action or inaction regarding the deed it has planned, inclines partially toward one side (i.e., any side, whether to commit or refrain from the act), the thought is known as an inclination (*hamm*). The thought at this stage merits reward if virtuous and punishment if evil.

ʿAzm

When the thought finally asserts itself and a decision is made to give it practical expression, it is known as a firm decision (*ʿazm*). Reward and punishment apply to this stage as well.

Signs of the Acquisition of a Relationship with Allāh Most High

Nisba literally means relationship or connection. A relationship or connection is a two-way process. It has two ends. In our context the relationship with Allāh means Allāh's connection with the servant and the servant's connection with Allāh Most High.

The attainment of a relationship with Allāh is also referred to as *wuṣūl ilā 'Llāh*. The relationship of Allāh with the servant is Allāh's pleasure with His servant. The relationship of the servant with Allāh means the servant's constant obedience and involvement in abundant remembrance with perfect awareness.

The sign of the existence of the servant's relationship with Allāh is his zeal to engage in obedience and worship as well as total abhorrence for all forms of sin and disobedience—both outward and inward. In addition to this is the servant's continuous determination to follow the Sunna.

Among the various kinds of worship, prayer is an all-embracing form. If executed properly, abiding by all its rules, conditions, and etiquette, then no other specific form of spiritual exercise is necessary for spiritual progress and the achievement of a relationship with Allāh. Prayer contains remembrance, spiritual exercise, meditation, *awrād*—glorification, asking forgiveness, blessings upon the Prophet (Allāh bless him and give him peace), and so forth. The remembrance of prayer is the recitation of the Qur'ān in it. This is in fact the highest form of remembrance. Spiritual exercise in prayer is the mind's preoccupation upon focusing the attention on the spot of prostration while standing, on the feet while bowing, on the bridge of the nose during prostration, on the lap in the sitting, and on the shoulders when saying the closing *salāms*.

Meditation in prayer is one's contemplation at the time of the opening *takbīr* [*Allāhu akbar*] and keeping in mind for the whole duration of prayer that "Allāh is watching me." This condition of total contemplation is called perfection or beautification (*iḥsān*). All spiritual struggle and exercises are undertaken to achieve this condition of perfection. Regarding the condition of perfection, a ḥadīth says that Jibrīl (peace be upon him) asked the Messenger of Allāh (Allāh bless him and give him peace), "What is perfection (*iḥsān*)?" The Messenger of Allāh (Allāh bless him and give him peace) replied, "That you worship Allāh as if you see Him, for though you do not see Him, [know] that He does see you" (*Muslim*).

In brief, the path of *sulūk* and its final destination, the stage of perfection, is attainable by fulfilling the prayer with all its etiquette, recommended acts, and conditions. In this way, the effects of the six spiritual faculties will become manifest.

The Six Spiritual Faculties and Their Effects

The six spiritual faculties (*al-laṭā'if al-sitta*) in man are the lower self (*nafs*), heart (*qalb*), spirit (*rūḥ*), secret (*sirr*), the hidden (*khafī*), and yet more hidden (*akhfā*). Their effects are as follows:

1. The lower self [that is well content]—its nourishment is abstention from sin and evil.
2. The heart—its nourishment is remembrance.
3. The spirit—its nourishment is constant alertness [in the presence of Allāh Most High].
4. The secret—its nourishment is the unveiling of realities.
5. The hidden—its nourishment is witnessing [that is, to behold the truth and to contemplate it] and annihilation [total absorption in Unity).
6. The yet more hidden—its nourishment is annihilation of annihilation [that is, to be unaware of even one's stage of annihilation]. Regarding this faculty there exist differences of opinion among the authorities.

The manifestations of the effects of these six faculties take on the following forms in prayer. There are seven degrees of prayer: the prayer of the body, the lower self, the heart, the spirit, the secret, the hidden, and the yet more hidden.

The effect of prayer of the body is prohibition of sin. That of the prayer of the lower self is abstaining from relationships other than the relationship with Allāh. That of the prayer of the heart is abstaining from heedlessness. That of the prayer of the spirit is preventing the gaze from looking at others. That of the prayer of the secret is preventing the mind from wandering and turning to others besides Allāh. That of the prayer of the hidden is man's achieving the degree of spiritual development where reality becomes manifest to him. And the effect of the prayer of the yet more hidden is true communion with Allāh Most High. The experience of this stage is [a form of spiritual] Ascension (*Miʿrāj*).

Conditions for Permission to Initiate into the Path

When the shaykh sees in a seeker a constant yearning for spiritual reformation (*iṣlāḥ*) and steadfastness in this purpose and the seeker upon the path of *sulūk* reaches the junction leading to Allāh Most High, the shaykh bestows the mantle of representation of the pledge (*khilāfat al-bayʿa*) upon the seeker, who is then appointed as the deputy (*khalīfa*) of the shaykh.

The seeker attains this lofty rank after continuous and regular association and communication with his shaykh.

Sulūk

The journey of *sulūk* comprises two journeys: the journey toward Allāh (*sayr ilā 'Llāh*) and the journey in Allāh (*sayr fī 'Llāh*).

The Journey toward Allāh

This journey consists of two fundamental aspects. One is the purification of the lower self from egotistical ailments known as blameworthy character traits. Reference to this is made in the Qur'ānic verse, "Verily, he has attained success who has purified his lower self" (Qur'ān 91:9). And the other is the adornment of the heart with praiseworthy character traits. This is called *taḥliya* and also *tajliya*. In *sulūk* this acquisition is described as stages (*maqāmāt*).

When the seeker becomes grounded in the acquisition of stages, in the purification of the lower self, and when he has achieved proficiency in the ways and means of acquiring praiseworthy character traits and eradicating blameworthy character traits, then, upon his reaching the stage of journeying toward Allāh, the shaykh confers on him the mantle of representation and grants him permission (*ijāza*) to initiate others into the Path.

The Journey in Allāh

Upon having attained the stage of journeying toward Allāh, a special celestial radiance (*jilā'*) and light (*nūr*) permeate the heart. The heart then is at all times dissociated from all things other than Allāh. The heart is now truly occupied with Allāh Most High. In this high stage of spiritual development, matters pertaining to the Being of Allāh (*dhāt*), the Attributes of Allāh (*ṣifāt*), the Acts of Allāh (*afʿāl*), and the Realities (*ḥaqā'iq*) as well as relationships between Allāh and His servants become manifest. This then is termed journeying in Allāh.

In the realm of journeying in Allāh there are no limits. Progress is infinite. Progress is proportional and continuous in relation to one's ability, occupation with Allāh Most High, and casting aside all motives, irrespective of whether such motives pertain to this world or the Hereafter. When one has attained this rank, one attributes nothing to oneself.

The shaykh appoints the seeker a *mujāz al-bayʿa* [that is, authorizes him to initiate seekers and to attend to their spiritual affairs] after he [the seeker] has attained the stage of journeying toward Allāh. Sometimes the shaykh delays this appointment until the seeker has reached the stage of journeying in Allāh. This appointment by the shaykh of the seeker at different stages of development is a matter confined entirely to the condition of the seeker and the inclination (*dhawq*) of the shaykh.

Searching for Another Shaykh

There are various reasons that a seeker might search for a shaykh other than his own. The seeker might discover that his first shaykh does not adhere to the Sharīʿa, or that he indulges in innovations or commits major sins. The seeker might have no congeniality with the first shaykh even if he is a strict adherent of the Sharīʿa and the Sunna. The first shaykh might pass away. In this event, it will suffice if the seeker turns to another shaykh to perfect his spiritual reformation without him even becoming his student. The seeker may, however, also complete his spiritual reformation under another shaykh along with entering into a pledge with him.

Our precedent in this aspect is our master Ḥājī Imdādullāh (may Allāh brighten his grave). Ḥājī Imdādullāh was first given permission to take the pledge in the Naqshbandī order. When his shaykh died, he gave the pledge to our master Miānjī Nūr Muḥammad (may Allāh brighten his grave) in the Chishtī order. Ḥājī Imdādullāh did so because he had not yet attained satiation in the spiritual journey. Our master Miānjī also conferred the mantle of permission to take the pledge to Ḥājī Imdādullāh. Today, both Arabs and non-Arabs have benefited from the spiritual effulgence and blessings of Ḥājī Imdādullāh.

It is vital to remember that after accepting another shaykh, the seeker should never be disrespectful to his former shaykh, neither in word or deed, not in his absence or presence. This applies even if the former shaykh happened to stray from the Sharīʿa. Any such disrespect will prove calamitous for the seeker. [Disrespect stems from pride and arrogance, which are destructive. The seeker had acquired at least a few words of advice and learning from even his innovator guide. The seeker had accepted the guide as his senior in the same way as a son accepts his transgressing father as his senior. The sinning, transgression, and reprehensible innovations of the father is not a licence for the son to be disrespectful to him. Similarly, the seeker is not permitted to behave with arrogant disrespect to his previous shaykh, even if he happens to be a deviate. The seeker should pray for him and occasionally send him a gift. (translator)]

Obstacles

All sin and connections other than those with Allāh Most High are bandits along the path of *sulūk*. There are several things from which the spiritual traveler has to abstain. This is vital. If the spiritual traveler does not rigorously abstain from these aspects, his efforts and struggles will be utterly wasted. These fatal obstacles strewn along the path of spiritual progress are mentioned in the following.

The first is opposition to the Sunna. Alas! In the present age, customs and innovations are in great prevalence. Nowadays such innovatory customs are regarded as *taṣawwuf.* The Messenger of Allāh (Allāh bless him and give him peace) said, "Soon there will dawn an age over people when there will remain of Islam nothing but its name, and of the Qur'ān there will remain nothing but its script" (Bayhaqī, *Shuʿab al-īmān*).

The second is inadvertently becoming the student of an irreligious guide (*pīr*) and, in spite of the error in this pledge, clinging to him life long. When the guide himself has not arrived (*wāṣil*), how will he cause the seeker to become one of the arrived?

The third is association with females and young boys, and casting lustful glances upon them. It is narrated in *Jawāhir-e ghaybī* that a man, while circumambulating the House of Allāh, once uttered, "O Allāh! I seek Your protection from Yourself." Someone asked him the meaning of this. He replied, "Once I cast a lustful glance upon a handsome lad when, a hand from the unseen appeared and slapped me, causing the loss of my eye." Yūsuf ibn Ḥusayn said, "I have observed that the calamities of the Ṣūfīs are in association with young lads, in companionship with impious persons, and inclining tenderly toward females."

Lust for lads is [in some ways] worse than lust for women. Nowadays such unnatural practices of lust with lads are very prevalent. The act of sodomy is severely prohibited; the Messenger of Allāh (Allāh bless him and give him peace) said, "I greatly fear for my people the practice of the nation of Lūṭ" (*Ibn Māja*). In another ḥadīth, the Messenger of Allāh (Allāh bless him and give him peace) said, "The curses of the angels of the seven heavens descend on seven types of sinners. The intensity of this curse is sufficient to destroy the accursed. [The first of the seven types] is one who practices sodomy." The Noble Prophet (Allāh bless him and give him peace) repeated the above warning thrice (*Ṭabarānī*). In another ḥadīth it is said, "Allāh Most High abhors looking at a man who commits sodomy" (*Tirmidhī*).

Some people, although not committing fornication, are involved in the malady of gazing with lust. It should be borne in mind that the eyes also commit fornication (*zinā*). Few people exercise caution in this respect despite the fact that staring with lust is a stepping-stone to fornication. According to the principle of *fiqh*, "the means and agencies of the unlawful are likewise unlawful." So remember this, and understand it well.

The fourth is evils of the tongue. Speech in abundance, and claiming excellence and virtues, and speaking disrespectfully of the Sharīʿa or Allāh Most High are among the greatest of impediments along the Path. Some ignorant guides indulge in such evil use of the tongue.

The fifth is to engage in spiritual struggle of one's own manufacture in addition to the instructions of the shaykh. Such unauthorized prescription by the seeker is detrimental. Within a short while, the seeker will become frustrated and discard even the little that he was instructed to do by the shaykh. This calamity has befallen many a seeker. It was because of this pitfall that the Messenger of Allāh (Allāh bless him and give him peace) instructed the adoption of only that much righteous work that will not wear one down and produce frustration.

The Messenger of Allāh (Allāh bless him and give him peace) said in this regard, "Allāh Most High will not 'weary' and be 'frustrated' as long as you do not become weary and frustrated" (*Bukhārī, Muslim*).

The sixth is haste in anticipation of the fruits of spiritual struggle. This is also a great obstacle. The seeker sometimes, in his haste and impatience, feels that even after having made much spiritual struggle for a while, he has not derived the fruits thereof. The consequence of this attitude is that the seeker either loses confidence in his shaykh or neglects his spiritual struggle. This is indeed a great calamity that can befall the seeker. It is imperative that the seeker realize that nothing is achieved overnight. The selfsame person at one stage was an infant. Only after a considerable lapse of time did he attain youth. At first he was ignorant, and only after some time had passed did he become a learned man. Similar then is the case of spiritual progress along the spiritual journey.

In short, haste and anticipation [of the effects of spiritual struggle to become manifest] are by implication demands that the seeker puts to his shaykh. Such demands are very harmful. This type of seeker does not remain content with his shaykh. He turns to all and sundry for remedies. He is like a vagrant along the Path, and consequentially he loses the attention and favor of the shaykh. The seeker, in the final analysis, loses in entirety what he had initially desired so impatiently. His frustration and worry multiply. Outwardly and inwardly he becomes overwhelmed by harm.

The seventh is introducing deficiencies in one's confidence and love for the shaykh. An even greater calamity than this is to hurt the feelings of the shaykh and to harm him. Such action and attitude bring about the total destruction of congeniality between the shaykh and the seeker.

The Harms of Matters beyond Our Control

There are some conditions and qualities which are beyond one's volitional control (*umūr ghayr ikhtiyāriyya*). These are natural states and attributes in man, and their cultivation and eradication are not within the scope of his ability.

Among the obstacles along the Path are another two ailments that are so widespread that almost all seekers are involved therein. Even some scholars are involved in these.

The one obstacle is the seeker's concern to acquire attributes and states not within his volitional control. Among these matters are perception or experience of the divine (*dhawq*), longing (*shawq*), absorption (*istighrāq*), bliss (*ladhdha*), solitude (*waḥda*), the ability to ward off passing thoughts (*dafʿ al-khaṭarāt*), pangs of spiritual love (*sōzish*), divine attraction (*injidhāb*), and so on. These states and attributes are erroneously considered to be the effects of remembrance, exercises, and spiritual struggle. The inability to attain these matters beyond our control is considered to be the consequence of having been deprived of the fruits of effort, but this too is erroneous.

The other obstacle is the seeker's effort to eliminate certain matters beyond his control, for instance, the state of *qabḍ* (spiritual contraction), a profusion of passing thoughts, inability to concentrate, natural love of wealth, dominance of natural anger, absence of tenderness, inability to shed tears, the assertion of worldly sorrow or fear, and so forth.

Sometimes the seeker regards these natural and non-volitional attributes and conditions to be detrimental to his progress along the Path. He labors under the notion that because of the presence of such matters beyond his control, he will not be able to attain his goal. Failure to eradicate these non-volitional aspects is erroneously considered to be a cause for drifting away from Allāh Most High. The above mentioned are two obstacles that generally occur to the travelers along this Path. The common factor between these two obstacles is the pursuit of things beyond one's control. Both acquisition and elimination of matters beyond one's control are not within man's capabilities. One suffers adversely by pursuing [the eradication or otherwise] of such non-volitional aspects. One harmful effect of such wasteful pursuit is the implied confrontation with the words of Allāh Most High: "Allāh does not impose on one (anything) but that which one can bear" (Qur'ān 2:286).

Since these aspects are non-volitional, their acquisition and elimination are beyond man's power and capacity. Allāh Most High has therefore not imposed such acquisition and elimination on the seeker. But when the spiritual traveler considers such acquisition and elimination necessary for the attainment of his goal, he, by implication, believes that this attitude of his is commanded and imperative. But as said earlier, the Sharīʿa has commanded one only in regard to that which one is capable of doing. The spiritual traveler's attitude implies that the ability to do so is not conditional for the performance of a task.

This, then, is his confrontation with the Divine words "Allāh does not impose on a person (anything) but that which one can bear" (Qur'ān 2:286).

Failure by the seeker to achieve the desired acquisition or elimination of matters beyond his control produces progressive frustration, the consequences being physical illness that may develop as a result of constant worry. This in turn results in the omission of many devotional practices. Frustration sometimes results in ill temper. Others are then inconvenienced by one's display of ill manners. Preponderance of worry and frustration at times causes one to neglect the rights of one's family as well as those of others. Such neglect becomes sinful. In some cases, this frustration reaches proportions that drive the seeker to suicide. Thus, both his worldly life and his Hereafter are destroyed. Sometimes the frustration causes the seeker to lose hope to the extent that he considers acts of obedience and righteousness to be useless. In consequence, he ends all his righteous activities and reaches an abrupt halt in his spiritual affairs. Sometimes he becomes disillusioned with his shaykh, losing confidence in him. He then labors under the notion that his shaykh is not aware of the Path. Sometimes the frustration becomes so extreme that one becomes displeased with Allāh Most High, attributing one's failure to Allāh Most High. One then finds fault with the promises that Allāh Most High has made in the Noble Qur'ān regarding His aid to the one who strives along His Path. May Allāh Most High protect us from such a disastrous end.

Advice for Those Involved in Remembrance and Devotional Practices

Those treading the Path should strive to follow the method of the Messenger of Allāh (Allāh bless him and give him peace) in everything. Following the Sunna creates much light in the heart. Have patience when anyone says something that displeases you. Do not say anything in haste, especially in anger. Be very careful in the state of anger. Never consider yourself to be perfect or one who possesses excellence. Think before speaking. When you are convinced that in what you intend to say there is no harm, and in it is some benefit or need regarding the world or religion, then only proclaim it. Never speak ill even of an evil person. Do not listen to evil. Do not criticize any dervish who may be overwhelmed by some ecstatic condition and may be saying something that, in your opinion, seems to be in conflict with the religion. Never despise any Muslim even if he happens to be a sinner. Never yearn nor have greed for wealth and honor. Do not make an occupation of spells (*taʿwīdh*) and amulets, for the general public will overwhelm you (with demands for charms and talismans). As much as is possible remain in the company of those who engage in remembrance. Such association creates light, courage, and love in the heart.

Do not expend much effort in worldly affairs. Do not meet people unnecessarily. When necessity compels you to meet others, meet them kindly and display good manners. As soon as the need has been fulfilled withdraw from company. Remain aloof especially from acquaintances. Search for the companionship of the people of Allāh (the pious and saintly ones) or meet with such persons who are not well known to you. Harm from such people is slight.

If some spiritual condition occurs in your heart or some amazing knowledge enters the heart, inform your shaykh. Do not request your shaykh for some specific devotional practice. Do not inform anyone besides your shaykh of the effect remembrance produces in you.

Do not deceive nor beat about the bush when you have realized your error. Confess immediately. In all circumstances have trust in Allāh and present your needs only to Him. Request Allāh to grant you steadfastness in the religion.

Important Advice for the Spiritual Traveler

The first step of the seeker in the Path is truthfulness or sincerity so that the structure can be erected on a proper foundation. The shaykhs have said that people have been deprived of *wuṣūl* (gaining Divine proximity) because they have destroyed the *uṣūl* (foundations). Thus, the first step is the rectification of belief that exists between Allāh and man. Such rectification is obligatory. Belief has necessarily to be free of doubt, suspicion, error, innovation, and should be established by means of absolute proofs.

Once the seeker has made firm his belief in Allāh Most High, then it is upon him to acquire a sufficient amount of knowledge of the Sharīʿa. Such knowledge may be acquired either by formal academic pursuit or by inquiring from some scholars. This is necessary so that one's duties and obligations be correctly discharged. When confronted by different verdicts of the scholars, adopt the one in which there is precaution (*aḥwaṭ*). Always resolve to remain aloof from disputation.

It is then essential that the seeker acquire moral character from some shaykh. If he has no teacher, he will never attain success.

When he resolves to enter into the Path, then after performing what has been explained above, it is obligatory upon him to seek forgiveness from Allāh Most High for all sins. He has to abstain from all sin, be they outward or inward and be they minor or major. First, he must make his peace with those who have rights over him. The Path will not open up for the traveler who has failed to make his peace with people who have rights over him.

Then he should strive to reduce his relationships and worldly activities because the edifice of *sulūk* is raised upon the peace of the heart. When intending to emerge from relationships, begin with emergence from wealth, for wealth is a thing which diverts one from Allāh Most High and inclines one to it. There has never been a seeker who, having entered this Path with worldly associations, remained steadfast. On the contrary, his worldly encumbrances diverted him, separated him from the Path, and restored him to former connections. The meaning of wealth here refers to wealth that is outside the bounds of the Sharīʿa as well as wealth in which one is engrossed more than necessary.

After emerging from wealth, it is obligatory to emerge from name and fame, for fame is a great obstacle along this Path. Nothing will the seeker gain until acceptance and rejection of him by others seem equal in value. The greatest harm for the seeker is the desire that people honor and respect him. Fame is a fatal poison to the seeker.

When the seeker has emerged from wealth and fame, it is then obligatory upon him to make a firm pledge to Allāh Most High that he will not oppose any of the counsels of his shaykh. Opposition to the shaykh is extremely harmful. Among the conditions of this pledge is that the seeker not entertain any objection regarding his shaykh even in his heart.

It is then obligatory upon him to conceal his secrets, not revealing them even to his closest associates. But he should not conceal them from his shaykh. If any seeker conceals even the slightest of his condition, then indeed, he has abused the right of companionship of his shaykh. If the seeker realizes, either by himself or by having been reminded by the shaykh, that he has opposed the shaykh in anything, he should immediately confess his error to the shaykh and submit happily to any punishment the shaykh may prescribe. It is not proper for the shaykh to overlook the faults of the seeker. If the shaykh does so, he will be guilty of destroying the rights of Allāh Most High.

Overlooking faults here means to refrain from calling the attention of the seeker to such faults. However, there is no harm in the shaykh forgiving the seeker and not punishing him when he [the shaykh] has hope of reforming the seeker without meting out punishment.

As long as the seeker has not renounced all associations, it is not permissible for the shaykh to prescribe for him any of the special formulae of remembrance. It is obligatory upon the shaykh to first put the seeker to test. After having tested the seeker, when the shaykh's heart bears testimony in regard to the firmness of the seeker's resolution, the shaykh should stipulate the condition that the seeker resign with pleasure to the variety of circumstances produced by fate in this Path. The shaykh must take a pledge from the seeker that he will not turn his face away from this Path regardless of whatever overtakes him, whether it be harm, disgrace, poverty, sickness, pain, or anything else. Furthermore, the seeker has to pledge that he will not incline toward the ease advocated by his heart, nor will he search for an easy way out at the time of hunger and need. He will not adopt physical comfort, nor will laxity become his way. Concession (*rukhsa*) and laxity (*kasal*) in this context refer to those prescribed by indolence or one's personal opinion. Such concessions and laxity are reprehensible. However, concessions advocated by the Sharīʿa or adopted on the instruction of the shaykh are not reprehensible.

It is extremely harmful for the seeker to sit in the gatherings of dervishes (*fuqarā'*) and People of the Path in the initial stages. [He may witness them in certain states that would cause him confusion, or he may not know how to act in their presence.] However, if some seeker has indulged in this error, then he should adopt the following methods and attitudes. He should respect the shaykhs and be of service to them. He should not contradict them, and he should act in a way that will give them comfort. He should refrain from any attitude that will create a barrier in the heart of the shaykh from him. In the association with the dervishes (*fuqarā'*), it is obligatory to give preference to them and not to consider oneself a greater claimant to any right. Consider the right of every one in the group of dervishes to be binding on you. Do not consider that you have any right over any of them. It is obligatory that the seeker not oppose any among the group. If the seeker discovers that he (the seeker himself) is correct, then he should maintain silence. This does not mean taking part in the false acts (*bāṭil*) of others. It merely means maintaining silence after proclaiming the truth and not indulging in disputation. In disputation is destruction of time and clouding of the heart. Do not permit such differences to effect your other social affairs. A seeker suffering from the habit of excessive laughter, obstinacy, and arguing will attain no progress in this Path.

Outward abundance of *awrād* [specific forms of remembrance] is not of the etiquette (*ādāb*) of the seeker. On the contrary, this group [of seekers] is ever engaged in eliminating stray and evil thoughts and diversions and the heart's negligence. Their occupation is purification of character and not abundance of practices. Obligatory and emphasized *sunna* (*mu'akkada*) acts are binding upon them. They firmly adhere to these. That the heart remains in a permanent state of remembrance is superior to a profusion of supererogatory acts of worship (*nafl*).

After the seeker has established in himself permanence of remembrance [i.e., that the heart and tongue perpetually engaging in *dhikr*] and has preferred solitude over publicity, he may experience certain supernatural occurrences while sleeping or while awake or in a condition between sleep and wakefulness. For example, he may hear a supernatural voice or experience the revelation of some metaphysical reality (*ḥaqīqa maʿnawiyya*). If this happens, the seeker should not pay any attention to it, nor should he attach any importance to such events. He should not await or remain in expectation of similar experiences because all such events are distractions. They divert the seeker's attention from Allāh Most High. However, it is imperative to notify the shaykh of all such occurrences and experiences. Relating this to the shaykh will free the heart of the burden of such experiences.

It is obligatory upon the shaykh to guard the secrets of the seeker. The shaykh shall detract from the importance of such supernatural experiences. In other words, he will explain their insignificance to the seeker because all such events are trials.

Contentment and pleasure with these supernatural experiences are in fact deception. The shaykh should, therefore, alert and warn the seeker about the danger of focusing the attention on such insignificant events. The shaykh should encourage the seeker to aspire for heights far loftier than such experiences.

Among the rules of the seeker is that he move to a place where he can be in the association of a shaykh who happens to be a guide for seekers of the age. Such a move is necessary if the seeker finds no such qualified shaykh in the place of his residence. The seeker should then remain in attendance of the shaykh and not depart until he obtains the permission of the shaykh.

The seeker should not entertain the idea that the shaykh is divinely protected from sin (*maʿṣūm*). However, he should hold the shaykh in high esteem and if occasionally the seeker witnesses any transgression by the shaykh, he should not sever his ties with the shaykh on this account. However, should the shaykh perpetrate acts of transgression in abundance, the seeker should sever his ties with the shaykh politely, honorably, and respectfully. The shaykh should also not command the seeker to do acts that constitute transgression [in the Sharīʿa].

Among the gravest of calamities and misfortunes in this Path is companionship with young lads. All the shaykhs unanimously assert that the one who has become involved in such association has in fact been disgraced by Allāh Most High.

Among the calamities for a seeker is subtle and concealed envy in his lower self for brothers along the Path. He should not envy any of his contemporaries in the Path if they have attained a distinguished rank while he has been deprived thereof. He should understand that all affairs have already been predetermined.

Of the etiquette of the seeker is that he should not aspire for leadership, nor should he desire that anyone become his seeker or student. If the seeker, prior to the annihilation of the self and elimination of the calamities, entertains such desires, then in fact he is deprived of reality. His advice and instruction will not benefit anyone.

The structure of this Path revolves around the protection of the etiquette of the Sharīʿa, guarding oneself against unlawful and doubtful things (*mushtabah*), guarding the senses against the things prohibited by the Sharīʿa, freeing one's moments of negligence and connecting them to Allāh, and not regarding as lawful even a grain in which there is doubt, even in times of need, let alone times of comfort and prosperity.

The seeker is required to perpetually struggle in abstaining from lust and base desires. He who complies with his desires destroys his acceptance [in this Path]. The worst thing that can happen to the seeker is that he return to a lust or desire that he had shunned for the sake of Allāh Most High.

It is not befitting of the rank of the [male] seeker to accept the politeness or tenderness of women [and risk falling prey to his desires]. This has been the method of all the spiritual travelers of this Path. When it is prohibited to even accept the politeness of women, then to a far greater degree will taking means to [attract and] acquire it be forbidden. This has been the way of the shaykhs. Whoever considers this an insignificant thing will soon be faced with affairs that will bring him to disgrace.

It is essential for the seeker to keep aloof of the seekers of the world because their companionship has been proven to be poison. Allāh Most High has said that one should not follow a person whose heart Allāh has turned away from His remembrance. The people of abstention (*ahl al-zuhd*) are on a quest for Allāh's Proximity, and in this endeavor they spend wealth. The purified ones (*ahl al-ṣafā'*), in their endeavors to acquire the companionship of Allāh, expel from their hearts all creation in general and acquaintances in particular.

General Admonition

The Commander of the believers, Imām of the East and the West, our master ʿAlī ibn Abī Ṭālib (may Allāh ennoble his countenance) said, "I have selected from the Noble Torah twelve statements, and I reflect on these statements thrice daily. Allāh Most High says:

> Mankind! Never fear any devil or king as long as My Reign endures.
>
> Mankind! Never be worried about our food as long as you find My treasuries full. My treasuries never decrease, nor will they be depleted.
>
> Mankind! When you become helpless in any affair, call Me, and most certainly, you will find Me. I am the Bestower of all things and all goodness.
>
> Mankind! Be assured that I regard you as My friend. You, therefore, befriend Me.
>
> Mankind! Do not cease to fear Me until you have crossed the Bridge [on the day of Judgment].
>
> Mankind! I have created you out of dust, blood clot, and sperm. I was not without perfect power when creating you, so how then should I be without power to feed you? Why, then, do you seek from others?

> Mankind! I have created all things for you and I have created you for My worship. But you have become trapped in what has been created for your service, and you have drifted away from Me for the sake of others.
>
> Mankind! All creation desires something for themselves, while I desire you for your own sake, but you run from Me.
>
> Mankind! You are displeased with Me because of the desires of the lower self, but never did you become displeased with your lower self for My sake.
>
> Mankind! Worshipping Me is obligatory on you, and providing you sustenance is obligatory upon Me. But in most cases you are negligent in your duty, while I am never negligent in feeding you.
>
> Mankind! You seek future sustenance even today, but I do not desire from you the worship of the future.
>
> Mankind! You will forever remain in peace and comfort if you are content with what I have given you. If you are not content with it, I will assert the greed of the world over you. It will then cause you to run from pillar to post, and from door to door, like a dog, in utter humiliation, and then too you will obtain only what has been predestined for you.

Further Advice

A sinner who repents is nobler than a man whose worship is accompanied by pride.

The sign of the heart enjoying a connection with Allāh Most High is the heart's inability to find enjoyment in any relationship of the world.

Sleep with death under your pillow, and when you arise do not have much hope in life.

Never consider sin to be small. Regard sin as great. He who thinks slightly of sin has considered Allāh to be insignificant.

Guard the lower self at all times.

Abstention from sin is of greater importance than [plenteous supererogatory] worship.

A small amount of lawful earnings is superior to earnings which are in abundance, but unlawful. Respect is in contentment and comfort in abstention.

Sturdy patience is to be pleased with one's lot.

It is of the acts of courage that one acquires the knowledge of the religion; practice perfectly with sincerity, and be fully contented and adopt beautiful patience.

A sheep is nobler than a man who sacrifices the commands of Allāh for the sake of his desire, for the call of the shepherd is heard by the sheep.

The association of the pious is better than acts of piety, and the association of the evil is worse than acts of evil.

The non-existence of even a grain of vanity and falsehood in one is an aspect of gnosis.

The look cast without the intention of gaining admonition and learning is total neglect and a medium of disgrace. Freedom is obtained by trampling the desires of the lower self underfoot. Elimination of envy occasions the love of Allāh.

When speaking, speak the truth whether in anger or in happiness.

Three persons depart with regret at the time of death: a man who spent his life accumulating wealth without having realized contentment, a man who did not obtain what he wished for, and a man who did not prepare his store for the Hereafter.

Abstain from the companionship of a friend who causes you no benefit in the Hereafter. The friendship of worldly people is like something that has beautiful color but bad taste. Our master Ḥasan [ibn ʿAlī] (may Allah be pleased with him) said, "Never listen to music no matter what rank you have attained."

The knowledge of a man who prefers conversation with people to remembrance of Allāh is little; his heart is blind, and his life is wasted.

The least degree of harm that befalls a man who befriends the world is that Allāh Most High eliminates the pleasure of His remembrance and supplication from his heart.

The devil does not bother about the one who, in this world, is a seeker of the pleasure of the lower self, because such a person has himself gone astray. What purpose then has the devil in seeking him out?

Our master Shaykh Muhammad Wāsiʿ (may Allāh have mercy on him) was among the very greatest of the Friends of Allāh. A man requested advice of him. The Shaykh said, "I will give you such advice by means of which you may become the king of the world and obtain peace in the Hereafter. Adopt *zuhd* (abstention) in this world. Never have any greed or hope with regard to any man. See all creation to be dependent on Allāh. It is then evident that you will become independent of all [creation]. This is the meaning of becoming a king."

Ruin comes to a person from six avenues: weakness of intention regarding the acts of the Hereafter; obedience to the commands of the devil and striving in that direction; in spite of nearness of death, to entertain distant hopes and plans; to adopt the pleasure of people in preference to the pleasure of Allāh; to abstain from the Sunna of the Messenger of Allāh (Allāh bless him and give him peace) because of obedience to the desires of the lower self; to cite the errors of previous Friends of Allāh as proof for one's acts and to bury their excellence.

The sign of love for Allāh Most High is that one follows the character, acts, laws, and ways of the beloved [Messenger] of Allāh (Allāh bless him and give him peace).

These ten attitudes will prove greatly beneficial in this world and the Hereafter: truth with sincerity, justice with creation, wrath with the lower self, service to the saints, love and mercy upon little ones, generosity with the dervishes, advice and admonition to friends, patience with enemies, silence with ignoramuses, and humility with the scholars.

Stay among people, but remain aloof. Your body should be among creation, but your heart with the Creator. This will ensure that negligence does not overtake you. Beware of such negligence lest you conform with people in a way that entails opposition to Allāh and His displeasure.

The sign of proximity and love of Allāh Most High is shunning all things that hinder the love of Allāh.

There are two kinds of repentance: *tawbat al-ināba* and *tawbat al-istijāba.* The first is to repent of sins because of the fear of Allāh's punishment. The second is to resort to repentance because of shame for Allāh Most High. One's worship is absolutely insignificant in the presence of His Majesty and Splendor.

Every part of the body has its repentance. The repentance of the heart is its intention to abstain from the unlawful. The repentance of the eye is to not glance at things forbidden. The repentance of the ear is to not listen to evil and nonsensical talk. The repentance of the hands is to not raise them toward what has been forbidden. The repentance of the stomach is to refrain from consuming the unlawful. The repentance of one's modesty is to abstain from acts of immorality and from fornication.

A contemptible person is one who, despite his being ignorant of the Path of Allāh, does not ask about it.

People said to our master Bāyazīd Basṭāmī (may Allāh have mercy on him), "You are a performer of many miracles. You walk on the surface of water." He replied, "This is no miracle. Twigs also float on water." People said: "But you fly in the air." He replied: "This too is no miracle, for tiny insects also fly in the air." People said, "It is indeed a great miracle that within a single night you travel to Makka the magnificent." He replied, "This too is nothing. Sorcerers journey in a single night from Hindustān (India) to Mount Diyānand." People said, "What then is a miracle?" He replied, "A miracle is the heart's obsession with none besides Allāh."

Your relationship with your shaykh should be like the relationship of our master Abū Bakr al-Ṣiddīq (Allāh be well pleased with him) with the Messenger of Allāh (Allāh bless him and give him peace). He never contradicted the Messenger of Allāh (Allāh bless him and give him peace) in either religious or worldly matters. The shaykh should fit the description given by our master Junayd (may Allāh have mercy on him): "The Noble Qur'ān in his right hand, the Sunna of the Messenger of Allāh (Allāh bless him and give him peace) in his left hand, and he walks in the light of these two lamps so that he does not fall in the pits of doubt nor in the darkness of innovation."

When man considers his lower self to be despicable and contemptible, it is the sign of Allāh loving and honoring him. And when he considers his lower self to be honorable and when his defects remain hidden from him, it is the sign of Allāh's abhorrence for him.

The Exercise of Pās Anfās

For strengthening presence of mind, increasing zeal, and improving memory, one of the simplest and most efficacious exercises known is *Pās Anfās,* or "Guarding the Breath." This is a breathing exercise and its method is as follows:

Take a deep breath. When inhaling concentrate on the word *Allāh*. When exhaling concentrate on the syllable *hū*. Do this repeatedly.

In the beginning, practice this exercise in solitude until you feel a warm sensation. Thereafter, perform it at all times: while walking, sitting, and so forth. In all states, endeavor to establish this concentration. At first some effort will be required. However, after a short while one's breathing will be so conditioned that it will become second nature and will happen spontaneously without one having to consciously strive to do it.

Biographies

Ḥakīm al-Umma Mawlānā Ashraf ʿAlī Thānawī

by Ali Altaf Mian

Mawlānā Ashraf ʿAlī Thānawī, referred to by many South Asian Muslims as Ḥakīm al-Umma ("Spiritual Physician of the Muslim Umma") and Mujaddid al-Milla ("Reformer of the Nation"), is a towering figure of Islamic revival and reawakening of South Asia in the twentieth century. Mawlānā Thānawī was the "most eminent religious figure of his time, a prolific author, and believed to be the greatest Ṣūfi of modern India."

"He led a very active life, teaching, preaching, writing, lecturing, and making occasional journeys" (Naeem 94). The distinguishing mark and guiding principle that led to the vast success of his message was a remarkable sense of balance and straightforwardness in his speeches and writings. Mawlānā Thānawī was an exemplar of the Qur'ānic verse "And thus have We made you a nation justly balanced, that you might be witnesses over mankind" (Qur'ān 2:143). An astounding, comprehensive knowledge of all branches of Islamic learning was evident in his personality, explicated in his lectures, and recorded in his writings. The Indian jurist Qāḍī Mujāhid al-Islām Qāsimī said, "It is hard to think of an area of Islamic sciences left unattended by his writings" (Zayd 11).

His religious approach encompasses all aspects of the subject under discussion, and his viewpoints on different issues reflect a genuine, thorough examination of traditional Islamic thought. His acute intelligence, revolutionary method of training and teaching, love of Allāh and His Messenger (Allāh bless him and give him peace), organized management of time, broadmindedness, tolerance, and unique and fresh, yet conservative, understanding of religious disciplines has etched him a permanent place in Islamic history.

He will be remembered as a reformer of the masses, an exemplary spiritual guide (shaykh), a prolific author, a spiritual jurist, an intellectual sage, and a fortifier of Islamic tradition who, at a time when Muslims were physically and intellectually attacked by Western colonial powers, supplied them with literary and academic firepower in the form of his speeches, writings, legal verdicts (*fatāwā*), and spiritual training (*tarbiya*) to battle all irreligious influences of the Modern Age. Describing the great religious services and endeavors of Mawlānā Thānawī, Muftī Muḥammad Taqī ʿUthmānī writes, "The likeness of his accomplishments is not found in many preceding centuries" (*Ḥakīm al-Ummat kē siyāsī afkār* 22).

Birth and Upbringing

Mawlānā Ashraf ʿAlī Thānawī, named ʿAbd al-Ghanī by his paternal family, was born in the village of Thānā Bhāwan (in the Muzaffarnagar district of the Uttar Pradesh province of India) on the fifth of Rabīʿ al-Awwal, 1280 AH (August 19, 1863 CE). He was named Ashraf ʿAlī by the renowned saint of the times Ḥāfiẓ Ghulām Murtaḍā Pānīpatī, who was a maternal relative of Mawlānā Thānawī.

His family was well-respected and held an eminent position in Thānā Bhāwan. His father, ʿAbd al-Ḥaq, was a wealthy landowner, a devout Muslim, and a respected citizen of Thānā Bhāwan. ʿAbd al-Ḥaq was well versed in the Persian language, and although he had not memorized the Qur'ān, he knew the Holy Book so well that he would sometimes correct the recitation of the *imām* during prayer. Mawlānā Ashraf ʿAlī Thānawī's lineage can be traced back to the second Caliph of Islam, ʿUmar ibn al-Khaṭṭāb, a glimpse of whose intelligence, wisdom, foresightedness, piety, and sincerity was certainly visible in Mawlānā Thānawī.

As a young boy, he was zealous in offering the prayer (*ṣalāt*), and by age twelve, he was constant in offering the night vigil prayer (*Tahajjud*). He attained his early Arabic and Persian education under his maternal uncle Wājid ʿAlī and Mawlānā Fatḥ Muḥammad in Thānā Bhāwan and also memorized the Holy Qur'ān at a very young age from Ḥāfiẓ Ḥasīn ʿAlī of Meerut.

Traditional Islamic Studies at Dār al-ʿUlūm Deoband

In 1295 AH, Mawlānā Thānawī enrolled at the prestigious Dār al-ʿUlūm Deoband, from where he graduated in 1301 AH, after studying under some of the most erudite Islamic theologians of his time. Among his teachers were Mawlānā Muḥammad Qāsim Nānōtwī, Mawlānā Rashīd Aḥmad Gangōhī, Mawlānā Muḥammad Yaʿqūb Nānōtwī, and Shaykh al-Hind Mawlānā Maḥmūd al-Ḥasan. Mawlānā Thānawī's six years at Deoband were spent under the tutorship and guidance of God-fearing men, many of whom were the spiritual students of Ḥājī Imdādullāh Muhājir Makkī.

The spiritually charged atmosphere of Dār al-ʿUlūm Deoband, coupled with brilliant teachers and Mawlānā Thānawī's own intelligence and piety, together contributed to the excellence of theory and practice that was manifested in his personality. His literary life began at Dār al-ʿUlūm Deoband, when he wrote *Mathnawī zēr-o bām* in Persian at the age of eighteen. He possessed unmatched linguistic skills and mastered the Arabic, Persian, and Urdu languages by the same age.

Teacher of the Teachers

Mawlānā Thānawī did not have many opportunities to study under the founder of Dār al-ʿUlūm Deoband, Mawlānā Qāsim Nānōtwī, whose last year [of life] coincided with Mawlānā Thānawī's first year there. However, Mawlānā Thānawī mentions that he would occasionally attend the lectures of Mawlānā Qāsim Nānōtwī on *Tafsīr al-Jalālayn* (a renowned exegesis of the Holy Qur'ān by Jalāl al-Dīn al-Maḥallī and his famous student Jalāl al-Dīn al-Suyūṭī). The two personalities from whom Mawlānā Thānawī greatly benefited were Mawlānā Rashīd Aḥmad Gangōhī and Mawlānā Muḥammad Yaʿqūb Nānōtwī.

Mawlānā Thānawī said, "Among my teachers, I was spiritually attached to Mawlānā Gangōhī more than anybody else, with the exception of Ḥājī Imdādullāh Muhājir Makkī. I have never witnessed such a unique personage, one in whom external and internal goodness merged so cohesively, like Mawlānā Rashīd Aḥmad Gangōhī" (Alwi 51). Mawlānā Thānawī received much affection and spiritual training from Mawlānā Gangōhī as well. Upon the arrival of Mawlānā Thānawī, Mawlānā Gangōhī would say, "When you arrive, I become alive" (Alwi 52). Once Mawlānā Thānawī came to Gangoh to deliver a lecture. Mawlānā Gangōhī sent all his visitors to attend this lecture, saying to them, "What are you doing here? Go and listen to the lecture of a truthful scholar." Mawlānā Gangōhī would also send some of his students to Thānā Bhāwan to benefit from the ocean of knowledge and spirituality that was Ashraf ʿAlī Thānawī.

Mawlānā Thānawī was also deeply inspired by Mawlānā Muḥammad Yaʿqūb Nānōtwī, a devout theologian and a divine mystic. Mawlānā Yaʿqūb had sensed that Ashraf ʿAlī was an unusual student, endowed with extraordinary traits. As a result, Mawlānā Yaʿqūb would make sure to include the most intricate discussions while teaching this bright student. Mawlānā Thānawī, describing the lectures of Mawlānā Yaʿqūb, said, "His lectures were not ordinary lectures, but sessions in which one's attention turned toward Allāh. He would be teaching exegesis of the Holy Qur'ān and tears would be flowing down his cheeks" (Alwi 51).

Graduation and Future Scope

Mawlānā Thānawī graduated from Dār al-ʿUlūm Deoband in 1301 AH (1884 CE). When Mawlānā Rashīd Aḥmad Gangōhī arrived for the graduation ceremony, Shaykh al-Hind Maḥmūd al-Ḥasan informed him that on that day a very bright and intelligent student would be graduating. Mawlānā Gangōhī wished to test this bright student. Hence, before the actual ceremony, Mawlānā Gangōhī asked Mawlānā Thānawī the most difficult questions he could think of. His answers amazed and pleased Mawlānā Gangōhī (Quraishi 14).

At the graduation, the turban-tying ceremony (*Dastār bandī*) was carried out by Mawlānā Rashīd Aḥmad Gangōhī. The graduation ceremony of that year stood out from the past and was celebrated with great enthusiasm and joy by the teachers of Deoband. At this occasion, Mawlānā Thānawī, with some classmates, said to his teacher Mawlānā Yaʿqūb, "We are not deserving of such a celebration and our graduation might bring derision to Dār al-ʿUlūm Deoband." Upon hearing this concern from Mawlānā Thānawī, Mawlānā Yaʿqūb became incensed and said, "This thinking of yours is completely wrong! At Dār al-ʿUlūm Deoband, you perceive of your personality as very meek and insignificant because of your teachers, and in fact, this is how you should feel. But once you graduate and step out of this institution, you will realize your worth and importance. I swear by Allāh, you will prevail and become dominant wherever you go; the field is open and empty [before you]" (Alwi 53). After graduating from Deoband, Mawlānā Thānawī accompanied his father to the holy cities of Makka and Madīna. After performing his first pilgrimage (*ḥajj*), Mawlānā Thānawī mastered the art of Qur'ānic recitation under Qārī Muḥammad ʿAbdullāh Muhājir Makkī. In Makka he also had the opportunity to stay in the companionship of Ḥājī Imdādullāh Muhājir Makkī, whose spiritual attention, luminous personality, brilliant teachings, and excellent methodology of training prepared Mawlānā Thānawī for the great reform movement he was destined to lead.

Spiritual Training under Ḥājī Imdādullāh

The Messenger of Allāh (Allāh bless him and give him peace) said, "Make the company of *ʿulamā'* compulsory upon yourselves and listen to the words of the wise, for Allāh Most Exalted restores life to dead hearts by the light of wisdom just as He makes alive the dead earth by rain" (ʿAsqalānī 25). Companionship of a pious, God-fearing shaykh is necessary for each and every Muslim. Through the knowledge of books, one's external self is reformed, and through the companionship of a shaykh, one's internal condition is purified. Mawlānā Thānawī was greatly concerned about focusing on his internal rectification. During his studies at Dār al-ʿUlūm Deoband, he asked that Mawlānā Rashīd Aḥmad Gangōhī train him in the spiritual sciences as well. However, Mawlānā Gangōhī advised him to wait until the completion of his traditional studies.

Mawlānā Thānawī remained restless and sought a way to ask Ḥājī Imdādullāh, the spiritual guide of Mawlānā Gangohī, to recommend him to Mawlānā Gangōhī. When Mawlānā Gangōhī went on *ḥajj*, Mawlānā Thānawī sent a letter with him to Ḥājī Imdādullāh, requesting the great mentor to persuade Mawlānā Gangōhī to initiate him in his spiritual order. Ḥājī Imdādullāh put in a good word for Mawlānā Thānawī and then said, "All right, I shall initiate him myself," and wrote to Mawlānā Thānawī, "Do not worry. I have taken you under my own mentorship." When Mawlānā Thānawī read the letter his heart became full of joy. Mawlānā Gangōhī used to say to Mawlānā Thānawī, "Brother, you have eaten of the ripe fruits of Ḥājī Imdādullāh, whereas we ate his unripe fruits" (Alwi 52). Fruits refer to knowledge. Mawlānā Gangōhī and his peers received the spiritual guidance of Ḥājī Imdādullāh when he was still in the Indian Subcontinent, and Mawlānā Thānawī benefited from him in his last years. Hence, the training of Ḥājī Imdādullāh in the later years of his life is compared to ripe fruits and his earlier training to unripe fruits.

Mawlānā Thānawī visited Ḥājī Imdādullāh during his first *ḥajj* in 1301 AH (1884 CE) but could not remain in his company for long. In 1310 AH (1893 CE), Mawlānā Thānawī left for the pilgrimage a second time and, after performing the *ḥajj*, stayed with his shaykh for six months.

Strengthening Knowledge through Teaching

Fourteen years after graduation were spent teaching religious sciences in the city of Kanpur. Over a very short period of time, Mawlānā Thānawī acquired a reputable position as a sound religious scholar. His teaching attracted many students, and his research and publications enhanced Islamic academia. In these fourteen years, he traveled to many cities and villages, delivering lectures in hope of reforming people. Printed versions of his lectures and discourses would usually become available shortly after these tours. Until then, very few scholars in the history of Islam had their lectures printed and widely circulated in their own lifetimes. The desire to reform the masses intensified in his heart during his stay at Kanpur.

Eventually, in 1315 AH, he retired from teaching and devoted himself to reestablishing the spiritual center (*khānqāh*) of his shaykh in Thānā Bhāwan. Upon this transition, Ḥājī Imdādullāh remarked, "It is good that you came to Thānā Bhāwan. It is hoped that the masses will benefit from you spiritually and physically. You should engage yourself in revitalizing our school (*madrasa*) and spiritual center (*khānqāh*) once more in Thānā Bhāwan. As for myself, I am always praying for you and attentive toward you" (Alwi 58).

Mastership in Islamic Spirituality (Taṣawwuf)

A master of Islamic spirituality, Mawlānā Thānawī was "widely considered the preeminent Ṣūfī of modern India" (Metcalf 157). His approach to *taṣawwuf* was in complete harmony with the Qur'ān and ḥadīth. Accurately summarizing the approach of the scholars associated with Dār al-ʿUlūm Deoband, regarding Sufism, Kenneth W. Jones writes:

> Deobandis conceived of Islam as having two points of focus, Sharīʿa (the law, based on scriptures and religious knowledge), and the *Ṭarīqa* (path, derived from religious experience). Thus they accepted Sufism with its form of discipline and the role of the *ʿulamāʾ* in interpreting the four schools of Islamic law. The Qurʾān, the ḥadīth, *qiyās* (analogical reasoning), and *ijmāʿ* (consensus) provided the foundation of religious knowledge, but understanding them required the *ʿulamāʾ* as guides. Uneducated Muslims could not make judgments on belief or practice. The Deobandis, while accepting Sufism, rejected numerous ceremonies and the authority of *pīrs* who claimed sanctity by their descent rather than by their learning. Knowledge granted authority and not inheritance. Pilgrimages to saints' tombs, and the annual death rites of a particular saint (the *urs*) also lay outside acceptable Islamic practice. Among the types of behavior seen as erroneous innovations was any social or religious practice that appeared to come from Hindu culture (Jones 60).

The scholars of Deoband purified Islamic mysticism in the Indian subcontinent from all un-Islamic elements and practiced a *taṣawwuf* that earlier Muslims, such as Ḥasan al-Baṣrī, Junayd al-Baghdādī, and ʿAbd al-Qādir al-Jīlānī would advocate if they were living in the twentieth century. Pure, unadulterated Sufism is an important part of the Islamic faith. Dār al-ʿUlūm Deoband trained individuals to become rational scholars as well as sound practitioners of *taṣawwuf*. Through the Deoband movement, Islamic history once more witnessed the combination of the *jurist* and the *mystic* into a well-rounded Islamic scholar. In choosing "Muftīs and Shaykhs" as the title of a chapter in her well-researched monograph *Islamic Revival in British India: Deoband, 1860–1900*, Barbara Daly Metcalf emphasizes this beautiful combination.

Effectiveness of Spiritual Efforts

Imām Shāfiʿī said, "Knowledge is not what is memorized; knowledge is what benefits" (Nawawī 43). Mawlānā Thānawī's knowledge was such that it not only benefited its contemplator, but continues to benefit Muslims all over the world. The words of Mawlānā Thānawī would flow into the ears of the attendants of his discourses and then would strike their hearts, scraping away their spiritual rust. Muftī Muḥammad Shafīʿ, former head muftī of Dār al-ʿUlūm Deoband and later the Grand Muftī of Pakistan, after the partition of India, would sit in front of Mawlānā Thānawī as a student of traditional Islamic studies sits before his teacher. "He would closely observe Mawlānā Thānawī, and each move of his showed that he had left this world and whatever was in it while engaging in the study of his shaykh's appearance. When Mawlānā Thānawī would say something remarkable, Muftī Muḥammad Shafīʿ, who seemed totally absorbed in his shaykh while unconscious of everything else, would leap forward in excitement" (ʿUthmānī, *Akābir-e Deoband kyā thē?* 30).

Muftī Muḥammad Taqī ʿUthmānī says,

> Ḥakīm al-Umma laid great stress on prescribing proper remedies for the spiritual ailments of people. This cure was not to give them some sort of medicinal syrup or to engage in some formulas (*waẓīfas*), but his prescribed remedy comprised action (*Irshādāt-e akābir* 25).

Students and Disciples

Mawlānā Thānawī's students and disciples constitute a generation of leading scholars of South Asia. His disciples settled in all parts of South Asia and served humanity in many different ways. Among his famous disciples are Qārī Muḥammad Ṭayyib Qāsimī (grandson of the founder of Dār al-ʿUlūm Deoband, Mawlānā Muḥammad Qāsim Nānōtwī, and head principal of Dār al-ʿUlūm Deoband for over fifty years, from the early 1930s to the early 1980s), Mawlānā Muḥammad Masīḥullāh Khān (founder of Madrasa Miftāḥ al-ʿUlūm in Jalalabad, India, and a leading spiritual figure of the past century), Muftī Muḥammad Shafīʿ (head muftī of Dār al-ʿUlūm Deoband before partition and, after migrating to Pakistan, founder of Dār al-ʿUlūm Karachi, one of the largest academies of religious sciences today in Pakistan, and, also the former Grand Muftī of Pakistan), Muftī Muḥammad Ḥasan of Amritsar (founder of Jāmiʿa Ashrafiyya, Lahore, Pakistan), Mawlānā Khayr Muḥammad Jālandhary (founder of Jāmiʿa Khayr al-Madāris, Multan, Pakistan), Mawlānā ʿAbd al-Bārī Nadwī (renowned theologian and philosopher in India who taught modern philosophy at Osmania University in Hyderabad and translated the books of Western philosophers, such as Descartes, into Urdu and left behind many valuable literary tracts), Sayyid Sulaymān Nadwī (great researcher and the outstanding student of Shiblī Nuʿmānī who turned to Mawlānā Thānawī for spiritual reformation),

Mawlānā Muḥammad Ilyās (founder of the Tablīgh Movement), Mawlānā ʿAbd al-Mājid Daryābādī, Mawlānā Athar ʿAlī of Silhet, Mawlānā Shams al-Ḥaqq Farīdpūrī, Mawlānā Muḥammad ʿAbd al-Ghanī Phūlpūrī, Mawlānā Shāh Muḥammad Abrār al-Ḥaqq of Hardoi, Khwājā ʿAzīz al-Ḥasan Majdhūb (great poet and mystic, author of *Ashraf al-sawāniḥ,* a four volume biography of Mawlānā Thānawī), Mawlānā Muḥammad Idrīs Kāndhlawī (author of *Maʿārif al-Qur'ān,* a commentary of the Qur'ān, and *Al-Taʿlīq al-ṣabīḥ,* a commentary of Tabrīzī's ḥadīth collection *Mishkāt al-Maṣābīḥ*), Mawlānā Ẓafar Aḥmad ʿUthmānī (author of the twenty-two volume compendium in Ḥanafī Law, *Iʿlā' al-Sunan)*, Muftī Jamīl Aḥmad Thānawī, Mawlānā Shabbīr ʿAlī Thānawī, Dr. ʿAbd al-Ḥayy ʿĀrifī, Mawlānā Muḥammad ʿĪsā of Allahabad, Mawlānā ʿAbd al-Ḥamīd of North Waziristan, Mawlānā ʿAbd al-Salām of Nawshehra, Mawlānā Muḥammad Saʿīd of Madras, Mawlānā Waṣī'ullāh of Fatehpur, Mawlānā ʿAbd al-Raḥmān Kāmilpūrī, Mawlānā Jalīl Aḥmad of Aligarh, Mawlānā Murtaḍā Ḥasan of Chandpur, Mawlānā Asadullāh of Rampur (head principal of Madrasa Maẓāhir ʿUlūm in Saharanpur for many years), Mawlānā Faqīr Muḥammad of Peshawar, Mawlānā Muḥammad Yūsuf Binnōrī (author of *Maʿārif al-Sunan,* a commentary on the *Sunan* of Imām Tirmidhī), Mawlānā Muḥammad Naʿīm of Kabul, and Muftī ʿAbd al-Karīm of Gamthla.

Literary Contributions

Mawlānā Thānawī was a prolific author. His literary contributions "range from 800 to 1000 in the shape of sermons, discussions, discourses, treatises, and books of high standard and quality" (Khwājā vii). Sayyid Sulaymān Nadwī said, "Mawlānā Thānawī was a translator and exegete (*mufassir*) of the Qur'ān. He explained its injunctions and wisdoms. He removed doubts and answered questions pertaining to the Qur'ān. Mawlānā Thānawī was a scholar of ḥadīth (*muḥaddith*) and expounded its intricacies and subtleties. He was a jurist (*faqīh*) who issued thousands of legal rulings (*fatāwā*). He solved many legal problems in contemporary issues in Islamic jurisprudence and answered them with the utmost caution and credible research. He was a moving orator (*khaṭīb*) whose speech was infused with all skills of oration. He was an excellent admonisher (*wāʿiẓ*) and hundreds of his speeches have been published and widely circulated.

Mawlānā Thānawī was a mystic (Ṣūfī) who revealed the secrets and subtleties of Islamic mysticism. His personality put an end to the battle that had been going on for some time between Sharīʿa and *taṣawwuf* by unifying these two essential parts of Islam" (Alwi 293). His books answered the objections raised against Islam by Orientalists and Modernists. "[His] analysis and refutation of the principles of modernism is not a merely theoretical exercise, but is meant to remove the obstacles to intellectual and spiritual understanding and growth for the pious and practicing Muslim" (Naeem 81).

His Arabic writings include *Sabq al-ghāyāt fī nasaq al-āyāt, Anwār al-Wujūd, Al-Tajallī wa 'l-aẓīm, Ḥawāshī Tafsīr Bayān al-Qur'ān, Taṣwīr al-muqaṭṭaʿāt, Al-Talkhīṣāt al-ʿashar, Mi'at durūs, Al-Khuṭab al-ma'thūra, Wujūh al-Mathānī, Ziyādāt, Jāmiʿ al-Āthār,* and *Ta'yīd al-Ḥaqīqa.*

Among his Persian books are *Mathnawī zēr-ō bām, Taʿlīqat-e Fārsī, ʿAqā'id baniy-e kālij.*

The rest of his books were written in the Urdu language, the most famous of which is *Behishtī Zēwar* [Heavenly Ornaments], which has become a handbook for leading an Islamic life in the Muslim household. Although Mawlānā Thānawī was the most prolific author of his times, he did not use any of his books as a source of income.

Qur'ān: The Special Interest of Mawlānā Thānawī

During his teaching career at Kanpur, Mawlānā Thānawī is reported to have seen ʿAbdullāh Ibn ʿAbbās—the cousin of the Prophet (Allāh bless him and give him peace) and the leading commentator on the Qur'ān among the Companions—in a dream that indicated to him that Qur'ānic exegesis should become his primary task (Alwi 297). Sayyid Sulaymān Nadwī said, "He not only memorized the words of the Qur'ān but also memorized the deeper significance of these words" (Alwi 297). He further said, "He was an exceptional reciter (*qārī*) of the Qur'ān who had mastered the art of recitation.... The uniqueness of Mawlānā Thānawī's recitation of the Qur'ān was such that each letter was uttered from its proper place of pronunciation (*makhraj*). There was no imitation or overly exertive effort to make his voice melodious. He would rather recite in his normal voice, which was full of inspiration and absorbed in reflection" (Alwi 297).

Mawlānā Thānawī was also an expert in the various recitations of the Qur'ān. In fact, he compiled the famous narrations of the different recitations in his book *Wujūh al-Mathānī* and the rare narrations in his book *Ziyādāt ʿalā kutub al-riwāyāt*. Mawlānā Thānawī's books on recitation of the Qur'ān also included *Jamāl al-Qur'ān, Tajwīd al-Qur'ān, Rafʿ al-khilāf fī ḥukm al-awqāf, Tanshīṭ al-ṭabʿ fī ijrā' al-sabʿ, Yādgār-e ḥaqq-e Qur'ān, Mutashābihāt al-Qur'ān li 'l-Tarāwīḥ*, and *Ādāb al-Qur'ān*. Mawlānā Thānawī's profound knowledge and insight in the Qur'ān is reflected in his Urdu translation of the meanings of the Qur'ān. His twelve volume exegesis, *Bayān al-Qur'ān*, can only be appreciated by a scholar who studies it after having read more than twenty commentaries on the Qur'ān (Alwi 323). Sayyid Sulaymān Nadwī said, "His commentary relies heavily on *Rūḥ al-Maʿānī* of ʿAllāma Ālūsī al-Baghdādī, and because it was written in the mid-thirteenth century AH, it encompasses all previous explanations of the Qur'ān" (Alwi 299).

Like Jaṣṣāṣ and other scholars, Mawlānā Thānawī also wished to collect legal rulings from the Qur'ān in support of the Ḥanafī school. However, his increasingly frail health in the last years of his life did not allow for him to directly author this work, which he wished to name *Dalā'il al-Qur'ān ʿalā madhhab al-Nuʿmān*. Instead, this academic desire of Mawlānā Thānawī was fulfilled by three of his outstanding students and disciples who noted down his explanations of legal rulings and their extractions from the Qur'ān. This Arabic work of Qur'ānic jurisprudence, entitled *Aḥkām al-Qur'ān li 'l-Thānawī*, is available in five volumes and is co-authored by Muftī Muḥammad Shafīʿ, Mawlānā Muḥammad Idrīs Kāndhlawī, and Mawlānā Ẓafar Aḥmad ʿUthmānī. Mawlānā ʿAbd al-Bārī Nadwī said,

> When Mawlānā Thānawī extracted Ḥanafī legal matters from the Qur'ān, we would be astonished that this point was always in this verse but our knowledge could not grasp it. His explanations would remove the clouds [of confusion], allowing us to fully benefit from the brilliant rays [of knowledge]" (Alwi 303).

Mawlānā Thānawī: A Caller to Allāh

Preaching Islam and calling people to the way of Allāh Almighty was an essential part of Mawlānā Thānawī's life. He would be highly organized and plan his lecture tours well in advance. Thousands used to attend these lectures, which usually lasted two to three hours and some even up to five hours. Mawlānā Thānawī also undertook a visit to the area of Mewat, where Muslims were at the verge of disbelief. His first visit to this area was in 1922, when he visited Alwar. Mawlānā Thānawī also paid a visit to Gajner, a village in the Kanpur district (U.P.), when the Arya Samāj started to preach Hinduism among the Muslims of that area. Using wisdom and tolerance, Mawlānā Thānawī was able to take a pledge from the people there "that they would not commit apostasy" (Masud lv). To prevent the spread of apostasy, he wrote the treatise *Al-Insidād li fitnat al-irtidād* [The eradication of the evils of apostasy] (Masud liv).

Rooting Out Irreligious Practices

Every true Islamic reformer roots out the irreligious practices people perform in the name of religion. Through his speeches and writings, Mawlānā Thānawī battled against all evil innovations in religion and presented Islam as it stood in light of the Qur'ān and ḥadīth. Mawlānā Thānawī was deeply concerned about the ignorance of those Muslims who performed many unnecessary acts perceiving them to be righteous acts of religion. Hence, he wrote many books that dealt with this subject. His book *Ḥifẓ al-īmān* clearly explains the evils in acts such as grave worshipping, beseeching other than Allāh, believing in the omnipresence of the Prophet (Allāh bless him and give him peace) and pious people, and so on. Another work entitled *Aghlāṭ al-ʿawām* is an earnest effort to root out all un-Islamic rituals prevalent among people. Innovations in belief, worship, and transactions are condemned in this book. Mawlānā Thānawī's balanced approach places all religious injunctions in their proper place without excess (*ifrāṭ*) or shortcoming (*tafrīṭ*).

Embodiment of Humility and Simplicity

Muftī Muḥammad Taqī ʿUthmānī says that Ḥakīm al-Umma Mawlānā Ashraf ʿAlī Thānawī used to say, "I consider myself inferior to every Muslim at the present time and possibly inferior to every non-Muslim with respect to the future" (*Irshādātē akābir* 25). He meant that at this time, I am inferior to every Muslim, and inferior to every non-Muslim with respect to the future, because a non-Muslim may accept Islam in the future and become more advanced than myself. Mawlānā Thānawī was more concerned with rectifying his own self than correcting others. Once, when he had to deliver many lectures, he said, "Whenever I find the need of reforming myself, I speak on that specific shortcoming of mine. This method is very beneficial. My speech entitled *Ghaḍab* (Anger) is an example of this" (Alwi 131). Once, after praising Allāh, Mawlānā Thānawī said, "I am never unmindful of reckoning with my own self. Whenever I admonish a disciple of mine, I also inspect my own self and continuously seek Allāh's protection from His reckoning" (Alwi 131).

Mawlānā Thānawī and Politics

Mawlānā Thānawī was not a politician, Muftī Muḥammad Taqī ʿUthmānī explains, "nor was politics his subject of interest" (*Ḥakīm al-Ummat ke siyāsī afkār* 22). However, Islam is a lifestyle that encompasses all human activities and provides clear and complete guidelines for all aspects of life. Thus, at appropriate places in his speeches and writings, Mawlānā Thānawī does comment on politics and provides his useful explanation in that field. While battling secularism, many contemporary Muslims perceived Islam as a branch of government and politics. Mawlānā Thānawī proved, mainly using Qur'ānic verses, that political rule is only a means of instituting Islam in our lives and not the purpose of life itself. All modern political notions in contradiction with the Qur'ān and Ḥadīth would have to be forsaken, and the pure, untainted political thought reflected in the Qur'ān and Ḥadīth should guide the Muslims in organizing and structuring their governments (see *Ḥakīm al-Ummat ke siyāsī afkār*).

Death of a Great Sage

Mawlānā Thānawī toiled to reform the masses and trained a large number of disciples who spread all over the South Asian Subcontinent. None can deny that his efforts brought a large number of Muslims back to the true teachings of Islam. Mawlānā Thānawī passed away in his hometown of Thānā Bhāwan on Rajab 2, 1362 AH (July 4, 1943 CE). His funeral prayer was led by his nephew, the great scholar of ḥadīth Mawlānā Ẓafar Aḥmad ʿUthmānī, and he was buried in the ʿIshq-e Bāzān graveyard. Mawlānā Thānawī will be remembered for his inspiring, lucid, and rational writing, balanced approach, and reformative teachings. These still serve many Muslims today in helping them understand the Qur'ān and the Sunna.

Books Cited in Biography

Alwī, Masᶜūd Aḥsan. *Maᶜāthir-e Ḥakīm al-Ummat.* Lahore: Idāra Islāmiyyāt, 1986.

al-ᶜAsqalānī, Ibn Ḥajar. *Al-Istiᶜdād li Yawm al-Maᶜād.* Cairo: Dār al-Bashīr, 1986.

Jones, Kenneth W. *Socio-Religious Reform Movements in British India.* Cambridge: Cambridge University, 1989.

Khawaja, Ahmed Alī. *Maulana Ashraf Alī Thanvi: His Views on Moral Philosophy and Tasawwuf.* Delhi: Adam Publishers, 2002.

Metcalf, Barbara Daly. *Islamic Revival in British India: Deoband, 1860-1900.* Princeton: Princeton University, 1982.

Masud, Muhammad Khalid, ed. *Travellers in Faith: Studies of the Tablighi Jamaʾat as a Transnational Islamic Movement for Faith Renewal.* Leiden: Brill, 2000.

Naeem, Fuad S. "A Traditional Islamic Response to the Rise of Modernism." *Islam, Fundamentalism, and the Betrayal of Tradition: Essays by Western Muslim Scholars.* Ed. Joseph E.B. Lumbard. Bloomington: World Wisdom, 2004. 79–120.

Nawawī, Abū Zakariyya Muḥyī ʾl-Dīn ibn Sharaf. Tr. Aisha Bewley. *Busṭān al-ᶜĀrifīn: The Garden of the Gnostics.* Leicester: Al-Farūq, 2001.

Qurayshī, Muḥammad Iqbāl. *Maᶜārif-e Gangōhī.* Lahore: Idāra Islamiyyāt, 1976.

ᶜUthmānī, Muftī Muḥammad Taqī. *Akabir-e Deoband kyā thē? (Who were the Elders of Deoband?).* Karachi: Idārat al-Maᶜārif, 2000.

———. *Ḥakīm al-Ummat ke siyāsī afkār (The political views of Ḥakīm al-Ummat)* in *Islam awr Siyāsat.* Multan: Idāra Taʾlīfāt-e Ashrafiyya.

———. *Irshādāt-e Akābir (Sayings of the Saintly Elders).* Multan: Idāra Taʾlīfāt-e Ashrafiyya, 1998.

Zayd, Muḥammad. *Dīnī daᶜwat-ō tablīgh ke uṣūl-ō aḥkām.* Multan: Idāra Taʾlīfāt-e Ashrafiyya, 1994.

Mawlānā Masīḥullāh Khān Shērwānī

One of the greatest authorities on *taṣawwuf* of his times, Mawlānā Muḥammad Masīḥullāh Khān was among the senior representatives (*khalīfas*) of Ḥakīm al-Umma Mawlānā Ashraf ʿAlī Thānawī. He hailed from the renowned and distinguished Shērwānī family of Pathans, who are descendents of the Messenger of Allāh (Allāh bless him and give him peace).

Mawlānā Masīḥullāh was born in 1329 or 1330 AH at Sarā'i Barla, in the district of Aligarh, India. From early childhood, he had a unique desire to sit in the company of the scholars and pious servants of Allah. In particular, he enjoyed the close companionship of Mawlānā Muḥammad Ilyās, the spiritual representative (*khalīfa*) of Shaykh al-Hind Maḥmūd al-Ḥasan. Through this relationship, Mawlānā Masīḥullāh was introduced to Ḥakīm al-Umma Mawlānā Thānawī, whom he came to love and strove to emulate.

With such great people in his midst at such an early age, he displayed a penchant for worship unlike many other youngsters his age. He spent a great deal of his time in the remembrance of Allāh and supererogatory acts of worship. He was a paragon of piety and other noble qualities. His virtue, simplicity, and dignity were acknowledged by many who came into contact with him as a youth and as an adult. Modesty and kindheartedness dominated his personality.

His character was so excellent that he even gained the heartfelt respect of his own teachers, who themselves were renowned scholars. One of his teachers, Muftī Saʿīd Aḥmad Lucknawī, a great jurist and ḥadīth scholar, witnessed his life from early childhood. He said, "Since childhood, he has been a shining example of modesty, dignity, respect, forbearance, sincerity, intelligence, and other admirable attributes." Muftī Saʿīd Aḥmad had mastered many branches of the Islamic sciences and was Mawlānā Masīḥullāh's teacher in these fields. Yet when Mawlānā Thānawī passed away, he went to Mawlānā Masīḥullāh as a student of *taṣawwuf.* This act of Muftī Saʿīd Aḥmad only gives further credence to the spiritual nobility and status of Mawlānā Masīḥullāh.

Education, Teaching, and Death

After completing his early education in his hometown, Mawlānā Masīḥullāh enrolled into the famous Islamic institute of learning, Dār al-ʿUlūm Deoband, from where he would later graduate. While at Deoband, he passed many of his days in solitude, totally engrossed in his acquisition of knowledge. He had the invaluable opportunity to study under Mawlānā Ḥusayn Aḥmad Madanī, Iʿzāz ʿAlī, Aṣghar Ḥusayn, and ʿAllāma Balyāwī, among others. His training under Mawlānā Thānawī gave him exceptional spiritual strength, which quickly earned him a position of honor and respect among students and scholars alike. The year when Mawlānā Masīḥullāh completed his Islamic studies at Deoband, Mawlānā Thānawī awarded him authorization to teach the science of *tasawwuf.* Mawlānā Masīḥullāh became a spiritual representative (*khalīfa*) of Mawlānā Thānawī at the age of 21, an astoundingly early age to receive such an honor. Despite his youth, Mawlānā Thānawī listed him among eleven of his most eminent spiritual representatives. Mawlānā Thānawī was very confident in his methods of spiritual training and would often refer students to him for such training.

Mawlānā Thānawī assigned him to operate a small school in the village of Jalalabad, which in a few years became a thriving Islamic institution called Madrasa Miftāḥ al-ʿUlūm. Students would come from far and wide to attend this school, in order to benefit from Shaykh Masīḥullāh's knowledge and wisdom.

Mawlānā Masīḥullāh would spend the entire day in the service of Islam. After Fajr, he would take a light breakfast and not eat anything thereafter until Maghrib time. For the entire day, he would sit in the sitting posture of *ṣalāt* and teach patiently. His teaching style was simple and effective, and he would constantly say, "I am only presenting this through the benevolence and mercy of Allāh." He followed the Sunna in every aspect of his life.

He passed away on 16 Jumādā al-Ūlā 1413 AH (12 November 1992 CE) with the remembrance of Allāh on his lips. Muftī Muḥammad ʿInayatullāh performed his funeral prayer, and he was buried in Jalalabad.

INDEX

B

C

D

E

F

N

O

P

Q

R

S

Notes

Notes

Notes

Also by

WHITE THREAD PRESS

Provisions for the Seekers

The Differences of the Imāms

Prayers for Forgiveness: Seeking Spiritual Enlightenment through Sincere Supplication

Fiqh al-Imam: Key Proofs in Hanafi Fiqh

Imām Abū Ḥanīfa's Al-Fiqh al-Akbar with Maghnīsawī's Commentary

The Laws of Animal Slaughter

Absolute Essentials of Islam

Sufism & Good Character

WHITE
THREAD

UK ORDER FORM

Give the gift of

The Path to Perfection

to your friends and colleagues

Ask at Your Local Islamic Bookstore or Order Here

[ ] Yes, I want____copies of *The Path to Perfection* for the special price of £6.95 each (RRP £8.95).

Shipping and handling free. Payment must accompany orders. Allow two weeks for delivery.

My check or money order for £_______ is enclosed.
Please charge my
[ ]Visa [ ]Mastercard [ ]Switch

Name ______________________________
Organization ______________________________
Address ______________________________
City/Postcode ______________________________
Phone ______________ E-Mail ______________
Card ______________________________
Exp. Date ______________ Signature ______________

Fax (020) 8534 9191 or e-mail your order to sales@azharacademy.com
or order online at
www.azharacademy.com

Optionally mail completed order form with payment to

Azhar Academy Ltd
at Continenta London Ltd
Cooks Road
London, E15 2PW
(020) 8534 9191

Carefully cut here or photocopy page

USA ORDER FORM

Give the gift of

The Path to Perfection

to your friends and colleagues

Ask at Your Local Islamic Bookstore or Order Here

[ ] Yes, I want____copies of *The Path to Perfection* for the special price of $12.95 each (RRP $14.95).

Include $1.95 for shipping and handling for one book, and $0.95 for each additional book. Ohio residents must include applicable sales tax. Canadian orders must include payment in US funds. Payment must accompany orders. Allow two weeks for delivery.

My check or money order for $_______ is enclosed.
Please charge my
[ ]Visa [ ]Mastercard [ ]American Express [ ]Discover

Name ____________________
Organization ____________________
Address ____________________
City/State/Zip ____________________
Phone ____________ E-Mail ____________
Card ____________________
Exp. Date ____________ Signature ____________

Fax (309) 273 1844 or e-mail your order to info@whitethreadpress.com
or order online through
www.whitethreadpress.com

Optionally mail completed order form with payment to

Al-Rashad Books
3340 Hunter Parkway
Cuyahoga Falls, OH 44223
805 968 4666

Carefully cut here or photocopy page